Learning VirtualDub

The complete guide to capturing, processing, and encoding digital video

Georgios Diamantopoulos

Sohail Salehi

John Buechler

Birmingham - Mumbai

Learning VirtualDub
The complete guide to capturing, processing, and encoding digital video

First edition: April 2005

Published by Packt Publishing Ltd.
32 Lincoln Road
Olton
Birmingham, B27 6PA, UK.

ISBN 1-904811-35-3

www.packtpub.com

Cover Design by www.visionwt.com

Credits

Authors
Georgios Diamantopoulos
Sohail Salehi
John Buechler

Commissioning Editor
David Barnes

Technical Editors
Ashutosh Pande
Paramita Chakrabarti

Layout
Paramita Chakrabarti

Indexer
Ashutosh Pande

Proofreader
Chris Smith

Cover Designer
Helen Wood

About the Authors

Georgios Diamantopoulos was born in February 1984. Born and raised in Corinth, Greece, his scientific inclination towards computers was evident in his teenage years and he pursued his dreams by moving to Birmingham, UK to study Computer Systems Engineering in 2001. Early on in his course he expressed further interest in video editing and compression. Georgios graduated in July 2004 with an Honors degree from the University of Birmingham, where he is currently researching in the field of video compression towards a PhD degree. He has been involved with various extracurricular activities such as writing documentation for various video-editing tasks and developing a video quality assessment utility called Video Quality Studio.

I would like to voice my sincere gratitude to my family and friends who have supported my choices and dreams from the start. Through the constant and honest feedback of David Barnes, my editor in Packt, this book has been better shaped to be reader-friendly and I have improved my writing style. Last but not least, I would like to thank everyone who has contributed to my knowledge of digital multimedia over the years—each contribution has been of great value.

John Buechler, a.k.a. PapaJohn, is the prominent specialist in the community of Movie Maker 2 users (the starter video editing software included in every version of Windows XP). He co-authored *Movie Maker 2—Zero to Hero*, and wrote *Movie Maker 2—Do Amazing Things*. Other writings include a tutorial in *MaximumPC* and weekly newsletters.

Movie Maker 2 is a basic starter application, and John encourages using other software that complements it. Virtual Dub has been a core item in his toolkit since the beginning. His books and other writings routinely include it.

PapaJohn has a very active online presence, with over 10,000 posts to newsgroups and forums in the past few years. His www.papajohn.org website is an authoritative online reference for Movie Maker users. He moderates forums at www.simplyDV.com and www.windowsmoviemakers.net, and is a regular at the microsoft.windowsxp.moviemaker newsgroup.

He won the annual Microsoft Most Valuable Professional (MVP) awards for three years straight: 2003 through 2005, and was further acknowledged by a special 2004 Windows 'Winny' award for outstanding community support by Microsoft.

Thanks to Avery Lee for developing and sharing such great software, Christian and the community of VirtualDub users who support and expand it, and David Barnes of Packt Publishing for selecting me to write the introductory chapter. I appreciate being involved in efforts that help everyone learn more about today's wonderful digital video editing tools.

Sohail Salehi was born in Mashad, Iran on March 17, 1975. He graduated in Software Engineering from Mashad University in 2000. In recent years, Sohail has contributed to over 20 books, mainly in programming and computer graphics. He has written frequent articles for *0 & 1 Magazine*—an IT magazine from Ferdowsi University. You can find a complete list of his works at `http://www.sohail2d.com`.

In the past he has worked as the Chairman in the IT department of various universities including Mashad, Ferdowsi, and the Industrial Management University.

Currently he is working on IT training standards for the Iranian "Work and Science Organization".

I'd like to thank my lovely wife Ghazal, who supported and accompanied me in every single step during the writing of this book.

And I'd like to thank David Barnes, whose guidance helped me to improve my writing.

And finally I'd like to thank all of my forum's active members and moderators who filled my absence on the board while I was working on this book.

Table of Contents

Introduction

VirtualDub is an open source video capture and processing program. It might not have the editing power of software like Adobe Premiere, but as a quick way to process video it's hard to beat.

You can use VirtualDub to trim and clean up video before exporting to tape or processing with another program. With the right plug-ins, you can output your video in various encoded formats—ready to be distributed on CD, DVD, or over the Internet.

VirtualDub is popular. At the time of writing, visitors to Sourceforge are downloading it over 16,000 times a day.

What This Book Covers

This book is your step-by-step guide to getting the most out of VirtualDub. As the title suggests, we'll cover how to **capture** video, **process** it with VirtualDub's editing and filtering features, and finally how to **encode** video in an appropriate format for distribution.

Whether you've been using it for a while, or are just downloading it for the first time, you'll find plenty in this book to develop your VirtualDub skills, leaving you with higher quality, more effective videos.

Chapter 1 introduces the key world of VirtualDub. We'll see how to get hold of VirtualDub and install it, and learn about the various tools that complement VirtualDub such as VDubMod and AviSynth.

In *Chapter 2*, we'll study the process of capturing video—choosing and installing video capture hardware of various kinds. You'll find out what to look for, and how to set it up on your computer.

Chapter 3 shows how to use this equipment to get crisp, good quality captures in VirtualDub. You'll also see how to do some basic "pre-processing" such as cropping and cleaning graphical noise from the video.

With the capturing done, it's time to do some processing! *Chapter 4* introduces VirtualDub's processing features, and helps you understand the VirtualDub interface that will be your home for the next few chapters.

Chapter 5 looks at some basic editing techniques: how to cut, copy, and paste sections of video, and how to extract images from videos.

Chapter 6 is where the real fun begins, as we transform the look of a video using VirtualDub's built-in filters.

In *Chapter 7* you'll see how to apply some even more advanced effects using plug-ins.

VirtualDub makes playing with video easy, but there's still some complex science going on behind the scenes. *Chapter 8* helps you understand the complex and arcane world of video—so you'll understand those terms like interlacing, frame rate, PAL, NTSC, field bob, and colorspaces.

In *Chapter 9* we look at how to use AviSynth, a popular "frameserver", to give us great control over video processing by writing scripts that deal with video one frame at a time.

Finally in *Chapter 10* you'll see how to encode and compress your video ready for distribution—so plenty of people can get to see the great work you've done!

Conventions

In this book you will find a number of text styles that distinguish between different kinds of information. Here are some examples of these styles and an explanation of their meanings.

Code words in text are shown as follows: "NOCACHE does not prevent caching in AutoComplete stores, in history records, and other areas."

New terms and **important words** are introduced in a bold-type font. Words that you see on the screen—in menus or dialog boxes, for example—appear in the text as follows: Are you still there?

> Tips, suggestions, or important notes appear in a box like this.

Reader Feedback

Feedback from our readers is always welcome. Let us know what you think about this book, what you liked, or may have disliked. Reader feedback is important for us to develop titles that you really get the most out of.

To send us general feedback, simply drop an e-mail to feedback@packtpub.com, making sure to mention the book title in the subject of your message.

If there is a book that you need and would like to see us publish, please send us a note in the Suggest a title form on www.packtpub.com or e-mail suggest@packtpub.com.

If there is a topic that you have expertise in and you are interested in either writing or contributing to a book, see our author guide on www.packtpub.com/authors.

Customer Support

Now that you are the proud owner of a Packt book, we have a number of things to help you to get the most from your purchase.

Errata

Although we have taken every care to ensure the accuracy of our contents, mistakes do happen. If you find a mistake in one of our books—maybe a mistake in text or code—we would be grateful if you would report this to us. By doing this you can save other readers from frustration, and also help to improve subsequent versions of this book.

If you find any errata, report them by visiting http://www.packtpub.com/support, selecting your book, clicking on the Submit Errata link, and entering the details of your errata. Once your errata have been verified, your submission will be accepted and the errata added to the list of existing errata. The existing errata can be viewed by selecting your title from http://www.packtpub.com/support.

Questions

You can contact us at questions@packtpub.com if you are having a problem with some aspect of the book, and we will do our best to address it.

1

Introducing VirtualDub

VirtualDub is an unusual and interesting name for video software. Having used VirtualDub hundreds of times during the writing of this introductory chapter, I've come to appreciate how apt the name is. By selecting a video file and then applying a myriad of individual or grouped filters, I quickly see what would happen if I decided to go forward and capture the changes in a new file. Since I preview them and don't create a new one, I'm looking at a 'virtual' file—one being 'dubbed' from the source file but with the changes I want. It's so easy, quick, and wonderful that you can easily forget the long time spent in seeing such previews when you were working with video editing software. Such is the world of VirtualDub.

You may have heard good things about VirtualDub. You probably bought or picked up this book because you're eager to explore the topic. Or maybe you just bumped into it while browsing books about digital video editing. In either case, this is the right book.

If you're already dabbling in digital video editing, you may have VirtualDub for no other reason than it was a free download and you had heard about it, but you don't know how to use it. Hopefully you have a camcorder or a library of old videos and a yearning to try your hand at digital video editing. But you're not sure where to begin and can use some more knowledge and skills, especially with VirtualDub.

Millions of photographers, videographers, amateurs, and computer users are in the same situation. Many use their computers to retouch images, make slide shows, and even try their hand at non-linear video editing. Others are eager to learn and try.

The constant rollout of new digital hardware and software products is dazzling and exciting, but it can also be intimidating to those who don't understand the basics or need to develop their skills further. Continued education and skill development are critical to enjoying the editing process and achieving results.

Thousands of software applications and utilities are being developed and rolled out as commercial products, shareware, or freeware. Most are short-lived or used by very few. Rarely does new software gain global acceptance (from casual to power users) and go on to enjoy a full life of its own. VirtualDub is one of those rarities. That in itself is a good reason to explore what it's all about.

Started only a few years ago, it has emerged since then to global awareness, acceptance, use, and accolades. It has a significant community of users and has inspired or spawned the development of other related software products such as VDubMod and AviSynth. According to the statistics at SourceForge.net there have been over 17 million downloads of VirtualDub or its associated packages for the four and a half year period from mid-2000 through the end of 2004.

VirtualDub and related software products make up the world of VirtualDub and this book will either introduce you to it or help you develop your skills with it.

Don't expect to stop when you finish reading this book. With ongoing development and expanding usage, there may never be a final product. It's the kind of software that continues growing and evolving. Use the book to get the background knowledge of the VirtualDub world, develop your skills to become totally comfortable with the software, and from there follow and adopt future developments with ease and excitement. Keep this book in your library for continued reference.

Whatever your main video editing software is and your personal video goals are, VirtualDub will enhance your videos.

What is VirtualDub?

The main web page `http://www.virtualdub.org/` defines VirtualDub as follows:

> "VirtualDub is a video capture/processing utility for 32-bit Windows platforms (95/98/ME/NT4/2000/XP), licensed under the GNU General Public License (GPL). It lacks the editing power of a general-purpose editor such as Adobe Premiere, but is streamlined for fast linear operations over video. It has batch-processing capabilities for processing large numbers of files and can be extended with third-party video filters. VirtualDub is mainly geared toward processing AVI files, although it can read (not write) MPEG-1 and also handle sets of BMP images."

VirtualDub is an Open Source tool and freely available to all. Various software tools have their place in the VirtualDub world, and we will cover them to some degree in this book. Use those that best fit your needs.

My personal video efforts revolve around the world of Windows XP and its Movie Maker software: a digital video editor that, like VirtualDub, has a significant user base. Movie Maker is similar to VirtualDub in that it focuses on handling AVI files. I can do lots without leaving Movie Maker, but video editors are always looking for that something special in their next project. When I have that yearning, I often turn to the world of

VirtualDub to achieve it. It's been in my toolbox for years and I'm always encouraging others to use it too. I've written books and magazine articles on Movie Maker and publish a weekly newsletter. I try to keep my writings focused on Movie Maker but felt honored when asked to write this introductory chapter. VirtualDub is just too good a software package; writing about it is easy.

Besides providing great editing touches, the world of VirtualDub builds bridges and links for those needing to work with files from different environments. In fact, as I'm writing this chapter in one window on my computer, VDubMod is actively working in another, converting a file from a DVD to an AVI file that I can use in Movie Maker.

VirtualDub started with a Windows AVI base for computer-based work, but has been branching out to other file types. CD/DVD/TV systems use a different video format, standardized by MPEG files. MPEG-1 files are the standard for VCDs. MPEG-2 is the standard for SVCDs and DVDs. VirtualDub, with its roots in AVI files, can't open the MPEG-2 files of a DVD. VdubMod, however, can handle the file type.

You don't have to wait any longer to see what you can do with VirtualDub. Pictures are worth a thousand words and videos are even more so. Here's a figure showing a video of a bride and her attendants arriving for the wedding ceremony, with the overlying text being added by the **subtitler** filter—one of the add-on filters for VirtualDub:

It's playing in the filter preview window, which lets you quickly scrub through the video ('scrub through' means to quickly change the frame location by grabbing and moving that slider under the preview window) to see what the applied effect looks like at any frame of the video.

When you want to add some effect to a clip, and your primary editing software can't do so, check VirtualDub and its related software. You'll be pleasantly surprised.

The World of VirtualDub

We will assume you're a novice at digital video editing: you have never used VirtualDub, and know nothing of the world of VirtualDub beyond having heard about or downloaded it. When you're finished with this book, you'll know all you need to and more.

VirtualDub supplements your main video editing software. It can be used to do some simple editing, but it's more about what you can do with the filters that have already been developed and the countless possibilities for new ones. The filters are those included in the software, provided by third parties, or developed by you. The world of VirtualDub is wide open to use, learn from, or contribute to.

A **filter** is anything that changes a frame or multiple frames of a video. You can apply one or many at the same time. You select the VirtualDub filter(s), choose filter settings, and VirtualDub applies them to the frames of the input file as it makes (renders) a new file. The change might be the addition of text as you saw above, a color change, the addition of a logo in the corner, a rotation by a few degrees, cropping—anything you can think of wanting or needing to do to a video file. Some changes fix problems and others enhance the video by achieving your desired effect.

Software

Avery Lee, who later donated it to the public domain, via the Free Software Foundation (http://www.fsf.org/), started VirtualDub.

The General Public Licenses are designed to make sure you have the freedom to distribute copies of free software (and charge for this service if you wish), receive source code or get it if you want it, change the software, or use pieces of it in new free programs. Use this freedom to the fullest.

VirtualDub has been adopted whole-heartedly and developed further. Features continue to be added or developed and other related applications are being spun off.

As you read through this book, you'll learn to use VirtualDub as well as encounter two popular complementary programs:

VDubMod

Think of this as a super version of VirtualDub. If you can't do something with VirtualDub, try VDubMod. For example, if you open an MPEG-2 file in VirtualDub you'll get an error message about no video frames being found in it. Try this in VDubMod and it'll open fine. (This, however, isn't a guarantee.)

Each computer has many video and audio codecs on it to render or play an audio or video file. They work in the background, but sometimes there are software conflicts that need to be resolved. Dig in and try things—use all your tools and you'll sort those that work on your system from those that don't. VDubMod with its expanded set of features will help.

AviSynth

VirtualDub and VDubMod are applications you open as usual, and work with in windows. AviSynth is a bit harder to grasp as it works more behind the scenes. It's a frame server.

A **frame server** takes the video frames from a movie file and feeds or serves them to the software that needs them for playback or processing/editing.

You can use AviSynth in two ways. The easiest way is to simply change the extension of a video file to read .avs. Open such a file and the frames will be obtained by AviSynth and passed to the default associated player, such as the Windows Media Player.

The other way is to create a simple text-based script file using Notepad. Enter some commands in the script file, give the script file an .avs extension, and AviSynth will execute the commands as it passes the frames on. A very simple script is a two liner, the first one pointing to the source file, and the second one saying 'reverse'. When AviSynth serves the frames to the player or editing software, it'll be serving them in reverse order: an effect sought after by many, but perhaps not included in their main editor.

You can use script commands to do lots of fun and useful things.

Users

There are some great and very established online websites and forums to get the latest in software downloads, follow continued developments, and get support. Here are some:

* http://forums.virtualdub.org/, started in mid-2002, has over 13,000 members. In addition to the forums in English, there are ones for Spanish, French, and German. The overall administrator is the extremely active ChristianHJW.
* Donald Graft's website http://neuron2.net/ provides a source to download plug-ins for VirtualDub and AviSynth.

Doom9's forums at `http://forum.doom9.org/` include two for AviSynth usage and development, and another for VirtualDub and VDubMod. With the latest tally showing over 50,000 posts on these three forums, you won't run out of reading material.

- The official VirtualDub site page at `http://www.virtualdub.org /virtualdub_docs` provides comprehensive online documentation.

- The AviSynth site at `http://www.avisynth.org/` has information about filter expressions and all aspects of AviSynth, including its official manual.

About this Book

VirtualDub and related software are Open Source tools for capturing, processing, and encoding video. Most tools belonging to the VirtualDub world will be covered to some degree in this book. We realize that different people use different software as their primary video editors and encourage readers to use the tools that best fit their purposes.

As the options and complexity for computers and software expand and the user community grows with them, so does the need for good tutorial information. That is the main reason for this book.

The concepts of digital video are easy to grasp. A common theme is to get a digital camcorder, copy the file into your computer, edit it a bit, burn a DVD, and watch it on your TV. It's only while starting from scratch and going down that path that you realize the many details that need some knowledge, understanding, and skills. As you learn about VirtualDub, you'll also be learning more about your primary editing software and other utilities in your toolbox.

We'll help you understand the scope and power of VirtualDub by using impressive and practical examples.

The book will give you a working knowledge of the terminology involved, to understand more easily the online documentation and forum posts. Key terms will be explained clearly as you read them. We don't assume you already know the world of digital video and the terms it uses.

You will end up with the confidence and background needed to effectively use VirtualDub and its related software, and to experiment on your own or with the community of forum users.

Read this book cover to cover, perhaps many times. Use it for reference as you continue to explore what you can do with your personal videos.

Let's look at the icons you'll have for the installed software and then go into some basic information about them, including the downloading and installing.

Installation Preview

When you finish this introductory chapter, you'll have downloaded and installed VirtualDub, VirtualDub Mod, and AviSynth. The figure shows the new icons that will be displayed on your computer desktop.

The topmost icons open Virtual Dub and a test utility included with it (which tests the performance of your hard drive). This checks how well it can handle the demands of digital video work:

The icon on the second row opens VDubMod.

The lowest icon opens an AviSynth folder, not the AviSynth engine. Since it is the behind-the-scenes frame server, you don't start the engine from an icon. Use the icon to open a folder filled with the scripts you use to give commands to the AviSynth frame server engine. The engine stays under the hood and you call on it as needed by tweaking and opening a script. We'll look at the engine and some scripts a little later in this chapter.

About VirtualDub

VirtualDub is simply a great video editing utility!

VirtualDub's strength isn't in putting together the timeline or storyboard of a movie, but rather in providing a simple way to apply one or more filters to alter video, frame-by-frame. Many of the filters or their functionality may be absent in your main editing software, for example, an option to rotate a clip by 4 or 5 degrees for fine-tuning, instead of being limited to the 90-degree increments.

VirtualDub is free to download and use. The download package is small and quick to get, it doesn't really need an installation (just copy it to your selected folder), and it works extremely fast and well. It's hard to think of a reason not to have it.

VirtualDub started with the processing of AVI files in the Windows environment, and there lies its strength. As per its documentation, it can read (not write) MPEG-1 and handle sets of BMP still pictures. It can handle both types I and II DV-AVI files. However, it can't read QuickTime, MPEG-2, Real Media, or Windows Media file types.

VirtualDub ignores filename extensions when determining a file type, so renaming a file extension won't change its ability to open it.

What VirtualDub Can Do

So if VirtualDub isn't an editor, what can it do? Despite being focused on pre- and post-processing rather than editing, it has an impressive feature list. It is a useful standalone video tool and a great companion to full-fledged editors because:

- It can read and write AVI2 (OpenDML) and multi-segment AVI clips.
- It has integrated MPEG-1 and Motion-JPEG decoders.
- It lets you remove and replace audio tracks without affecting the video.
- It includes a wide variety of video filters: blur, sharpen, emboss, smooth, 3x3 convolution, flip, resize, rotate, brightness/contrast levels, deinterlace, and threshold. It also allows users to write their own video filters.
- It supports bilinear and bicubic resampling, which help avoid blocky resizes and rotates.
- It can decompress, recompress, and adjust compression of audio and video.
- It's great for quickly removing segments of a video, without recompressing the whole sequence.
- It can adjust frame rate, decimate frames, and perform 3:2 pulldown removal.
- VirtualDub can preview the effects of changes quickly, complete with audio.

You can take a captured clip, trim the ends, clean up some of the noise, convert it to the proper frame size, and write out a better one. Don't see a video filter you want? Write your own, with the filter SDK. In addition to these features, version 1.6.0 can use type I or II DV-AVI files as inputs, although it saves output files as type II.

Capturing Video with VirtualDub

For many users, video editing starts with the capture of video from a camcorder or other device to get the file to your computer. VirtualDub provides an option to do it, provided your device is compatible with Video for Windows. However, VirtualDub offers some powerful features that are rare in run-of-the-mill capture applications:

- Fractional frame rates. Instead of being forced to have a whole number of frames per second, VirtualDub will enable you to select (for example) 29.97 frames per second.

- Optimized disk access for more consistent hard disk usage.

- Create AVI2 (OpenDML) files that exceed the AVI 2GB barrier and multiple files to break the FAT32 4GB limit.

- Integrated volume meter and histogram for input level monitoring.

- Real-time downsizing, noise reduction, and field swapping.

- Verbose monitoring, including compression levels, CPU usage, and free disk space.

- Access hidden video formats which your capture card may support, but not have a setting for, such as 352x480.

- Keyboard and mouse shortcuts for faster operation. To capture, just hit F6.

- Clean interface layout: caption, menu bar, information panel, status bar.

The `http://www.virtualdub.org/docs_capture` page of the website has a number of tips including the following:

> "VirtualDub needs a Video for Windows capture driver to capture. Most Firewire (DV) devices do not provide a VFW driver, and thus cannot be used by VirtualDub at all. Also, ATI appears to be shipping their current devices with a WDM (Windows Driver Model) driver only; this can be used indirectly by VirtualDub through a Microsoft wrapper, but it is crippled in functionality and it also appears that the wrapper is buggy. The wrapper will show up as "Microsoft WDM Image Capture (Win32)". If it works for you, great."

You may not need VirtualDub to capture your video, as your main editing software provides such features.

VirtualDub's Early Development Years

In the days when Avery Lee created VirtualDub, previewing and rendering video was a time-consuming process. Many would say that this is true even with today's more powerful computers. One of Lee's goals was to make things happen quickly, and he achieved it. The software was designed for speed, both in its user interface and in the under-the-hood computer processing. You can easily see his results as you use it.

The `http://www.virtualdub.org/virtualdub_history` page at `virtualdub.org` gives us some insights into why Avery Lee started Virtual Dub, and some interesting information about it.

Ongoing Development

We'll use version 1.6.0 for the book. There are other versions available.

The latest experimental version 1.6.3 and its source code are also available for download and use, with information included about known issues.

If you intend to use the source code and do your own development, be sure to check the online information and support forums, including the pages at `http://www.virtualdub.org/docs_compiling` and `http://www.virtualdub.org/filtersdk`.

About VDubMod

As mentioned earlier, VDubMod is a super-version of VirtualDub. Whereas VirtualDub is the rock foundation and offers the ultimate in stability, much of the development into new areas has gone into VDubMod.

If you can't do something with VirtualDub, try VDubMod. An example is using an MPEG-2 source file. In VirtualDub you get an error message about there being no video frames in it. Try opening it in VDubMod.

Take the MPEG-2 example a step further. Put a DVD disc into your DVD drive, open a VOB file on it with VDubMod, and rip the video and audio to an AVI file.

This isn't a guarantee. Each computer has many video and audio codecs on it that are needed to render or play audio and video files. The codecs run in the background. Sometimes the right codec isn't installed or registered, and at other times software conflicts need to be resolved. If these issues are not effectively resolved, one or more programs could hang or crash.

After you have VirtualDub under your belt, dig into VDubMod and try some things you can't do in VirtualDub. Use all the tools you have, and you'll sort the ones that work from those that don't. A lot of your learning about video editing area is done experientially. Dig in and see how things go.

The introduction to the Help file says:

> "VirtualDubMod is a project that was born when suddenly a lot of modifications to the original VirtualDub by Avery Lee sprung up, mainly on the Doom9 forums. Some people got tired of needing several different modified VirtualDub executables, so the idea arose to put them all together into a single application, VirtualDubMod."

The founders were:

- VirtualDubOGM: Cyrius
- VirtualDubMPeg2: Pulco-Citron
- VirtualDubAVS: Belgabor

The Help file provides information about the extended features of VDubMod beyond those of VirtualDub, which include:

- **Preferences**: Expanded and include a new audio section.
- **AVI information**: Includes the FourCC code and the audio tag.
- **Image formats**: Uses the Corona library. This library handles BMP, TARGA, PNG, JPEG, GIF, and PCX image formats on input, and PNG on output. This means that you can open image sequences in one of those formats (BMP and TARGA are still handled by VirtualDub internal routines though), and save to a BMP (using VirtualDub BMP routines), TARGA (using VirtualDub TARGA routines), or PNG (using Corona PNG routines) sequence of images.
- **Streams menu**: Uses multiple streams in its standard use (for example when writing AVI files). The Audio menu was replaced by Streams in the main menu. This new menu lets you access features for the Video stream and the list of currently available streams (Stream list).
- **Multiple streams handling**: Manage the available streams thanks to Streams | Stream list. The window that appears lists all the additional streams presently opened in VDubMod (those beyond the video stream).
- **Comments and chapters handling**: Access specific comments or chapters for a stream using **Comments** and **Chapters**. The video comments and chapters are accessible thanks to Video comments and Video chapters in the Streams menu.
- **Previewing and saving**: A few things changed in the File menu.
- **Batch mode**: The job file will save all information concerning used streams and their options (compression), comments, and chapters, so you can still

use the Don't run this job now; add it to job control so I can run it in batch mode feature. Note that a Skip button has been added in the Job list window. Unlike Abort (which stops jobs processing), it aborts the current job and goes on to the next one. Also your current configuration (input streams selected and their associated comments and chapters) can be saved using Save processing settings, and can be reloaded using Load processing settings.

- **Miscellanea**: The Go to last keyframe feature was added in the Edit menu. This feature lets you jump to the nearest previous key frame preceding a certain position (expressed in megabytes) in the file.

We'll get into downloading and installing VDubMod after taking a summary look at the features of AviSynth.

About AviSynth

The documentation included with AviSynth provides this answer to "What is AviSynth?"

AviSynth (AVI SYNTHesizer) is a frame server. This means that it serves up video, frame by frame, to another video application. The core of AviSynth's power is scripting. Scripts are simple text files that contain a set of commands referencing one or more videos, and the effects you want to run on them.

When you open these script files in VirtualDub or another video application, AviSynth takes action. AviSynth performs the commands in the script, and sends the resulting video—frame by frame—to the video application. The video application has no idea what AviSynth is doing. As far as the application is concerned, it's opened a standard AVI file with all the filters and other commands already applied.

There are five main reasons why people would want to use AviSynth:

1. AviSynth can **join videos** together on the fly, or otherwise combine media from two sources (for example dubbing a new soundtrack).
2. AviSynth has a lot of support for **filtering video**, including built-in filters for resizing, cropping, and sharpening.
3. Many programs do not support video files larger than 2GB. By using AviSynth as the 'middle-man' between your video application and the video file, you can **break the 2GB barrier**.
4. AviSynth can make just about any type of video look like a normal AVI, including MPEGs and some Quicktime MOVs. Therefore, AviSynth is an easy way to get applications to open **unsupported video formats**.
5. AviSynth scripts take up only a small amount of disc space, yet can seem like completely new videos. Because the filtering and joining take place on the

fly, there is **no need to waste disk space** on temporary files or intermediate videos.

As VirtualDub users, our main interest with AviSynth will be applying filters. But the disk space savings are also a handy feature for the heavy VirtualDubber.

Let's move on to downloading and installing these three software packages from the world of VirtualDub. We'll do VirtualDub first, followed by VDubMod and AviSynth.

Downloading and Installing VirtualDub

The download is a zipped package of size less then a megabyte. Get it from the official website at http://www.virtualdub.org/, or for v1.6.0 from this link at SourceForge.net: http://prdownloads.sourceforge.net/virtualdub/VirtualDub-1.6.0.zip?use_mirror=optusnet. The file name includes the version number, so your downloaded file will be something like VirtualDub-1.6.0.zip.

Install by extracting the zipped files to any folder. An installation process isn't required. You can use WinZip to extract files from the zipped package, available from http://www.winzip.com/.

Be sure to tell the unzip utility to include folders in the unzip operation as some of the files need to be in their own folder. The following figure shows the files and subfolders you'll have:

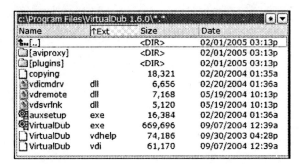

One of the subfolders is named plugins. This contains all filter files. Let's drill down into it and install a few filters.

Additional Filters

You can download and add additional filters to the 30 included in the basic VirtualDub software. They are available from Donald Graft's website at http://neuron2.net/.

Load a VirtualDub filter manually by clicking on the Load button that appears in the Add Filters dialog box. You can also have them automatically loaded at the startup of VirtualDub by copying the .vdf files into the plugins subfolder.

A few of the available filters are:

- **Deshaker**: Takes the unplanned shakes out of your recorded footage. Download the Deshaker.zip file from http://home.bip.net/gunnart/video/Deshaker.zip and copy the deshaker.vdf filter file to the plugins folder.

- **Subtitler**: Overlays text on a video. The text is defined in an SSA script file. You can use different size fonts, colors, and positioning.

- **Delogo**: Removes an embedded logo or timestamp by changing the selected area such that the pixels blend into the surrounding ones. The filter is available from http://neuron2.net/delogo132/delogo.html.

- **Warpsharp**: Tightens edges in an image by warping the image toward edge boundaries.

Filters have an extension of .vdf (VirtualDub filter). The following figure shows a few of them in the plugins folder:

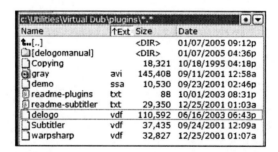

Copying the filter file from a downloaded zip file to the plugins subfolder is all that is needed to use it. The delogo filter comes with a complete instruction manual, which we've placed in a delogomanual subfolder.

The next figure shows the delogo filter being applied to remove the time stamp from a video that inadvertently included it in the recording. Not only was it in the video, but the monorail in Seattle was running on Pacific Time while the camcorder was on Eastern, so it was three hours off:

It's unusual but possible for filters to conflict with each other. If you have problems with a particular group of filters, check them individually and change the sequence they are applied in.

VirtualDub Source Code

If you're curious about the source code and how VirtualDub works, or want to try your hand at developing it further, the source code packages are a download away, in files packed using the **bzip2** block-sorting compressor. The links to the latest stable and developmental releases are:

```
http://prdownloads.sourceforge.net/virtualdub/VirtualDub-1.6.0-
src.zip.bz2?download
```

```
http://prdownloads.sourceforge.net/virtualdub/VirtualDub-1.6.3-
src.zip.bz2?download
```

You can extract the files from the 1+ MB packages using a utility such as WinRAR, available from `http://www.rarlab.com/`.

This codebase will build both normal and P4 versions. All tools necessary to build the release executable and help file are included (verinc, mapconv, disasm, and Lina).

You'll need Microsoft Visual C++ 6.0 Service Pack 5 + Processor Pack or later to build the general release, and Intel C/C++ 6.0 or later to build the P4 version.

And, as with other aspects of VirtualDub, the source code to study how the filters work or develop them further is also available for download.

Downloading and Installing VDubMod

Download VDubMod from `http://www.free-codecs.com/download/VirtualDubMod.htm`.

The `VirtualDubMod_1_5_10_1_All_inclusive.zip` file is about twice as large as the VirtualDub download file. It's bigger because it's all of what's in Virtual Dub and more.

Extract it from its zipped file and install as you did VirtualDub, placing the files and subfolders in any folder. An installation process isn't included or needed. The following figure shows the files and subfolders you'll have:

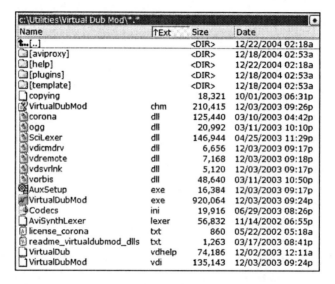

Name	↑Ext	Size	Date
[..]		<DIR>	12/22/2004 02:18a
[aviproxy]		<DIR>	12/18/2004 02:53a
[help]		<DIR>	12/22/2004 02:18a
[plugins]		<DIR>	12/18/2004 02:53a
[template]		<DIR>	12/18/2004 02:53a
copying		18,321	10/01/2003 06:31p
VirtualDubMod	chm	210,415	12/03/2003 09:26p
corona	dll	125,440	03/10/2003 04:42p
ogg	dll	20,992	03/11/2003 10:10p
SciLexer	dll	146,944	04/25/2003 11:29p
vdicmdrv	dll	6,656	12/03/2003 09:17p
vdremote	dll	7,168	12/03/2003 09:18p
vdsvrlnk	dll	5,120	12/03/2003 09:17p
vorbis	dll	48,640	03/11/2003 10:50p
AuxSetup	exe	16,384	12/03/2003 09:17p
VirtualDubMod	exe	920,064	12/03/2003 09:24p
Codecs	ini	19,916	06/29/2003 08:26p
AviSynthLexer	lexer	56,832	11/14/2002 06:55p
license_corona	txt	860	05/22/2002 05:18a
readme_virtualdubmod_dlls	txt	1,263	03/17/2003 08:41p
VirtualDub	vdhelp	74,186	12/02/2003 12:11a
VirtualDubMod	vdi	135,143	12/03/2003 09:24p

Downloading and Installing AviSynth

Download AviSynth from `http://sourceforge.net/projects/avisynth2/`.
The downloaded file is a self-extracting/self-installing executable, not a zipped one like VirtualDub.

Open or run it after downloading to do the installation. It'll offer you a few options, as shown in the following figure:

- Documentation in any or all of English, German, and French.

- Associating the AVS script files with Notepad (for editing) and/or Media Player 6.4 (the default viewer). Choose it and change it later if you want to.

- A destination folder to install the folders and files: by default the `C:\Program Files\AviSynth 2.5`.

Choose your options and the auto install takes only a minute:

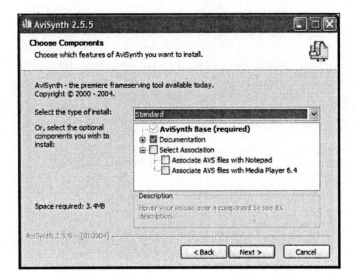

The installation process installs the following:

The frame server engine: the AviSynth.dll file is placed in the c:\Windows\System32 folder. The following figure shows the DLL and one of the pages of its properties:

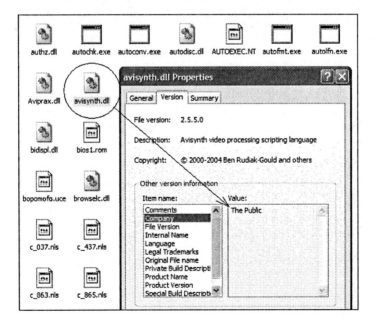

Looking at the Company name on the version tab shows who owns it—The Public. You do.

The frame-server engine, the DLL, will automatically go to work when you call on it by opening an AVS file. You've seen how it takes the frames from a source video file, processes the filters and actions applied by a script, and feeds the modified frames to an application for viewing or further processing.

The other files: The next figure shows the folders for AviSynth, and the files in its Examples subfolder, a good place to start:

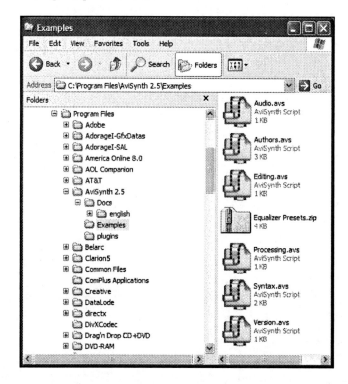

Remember that your job is to call on the frame-server engine by either renaming a video file to give it an .avs extension, or making an AVS script with commands in it.

If you rename a video file, just add .avs after the original extension so you'll remember what to change it back to. A renamed file might read: video.avi.avs. It might look like a double extension, but Windows will use the last part of the file name to determine which program to open it with.

All six example scripts in the folder are included in the download package. Check the engine and script processing by double-clicking or opening the Authors.avs sample file. The Windows Media Player will open and play the script file as if it were a video.

The following figure shows a snapshot of what you'll see: scrolling credits with rainbow-colored background and music. This sample is being played with the default version 6.4 Windows Media Player in Windows XP.

Look inside the script and you'll find there's no source video file involved. What you're seeing in the player is completely the result of script commands. Tweak the script and put your own text in it:

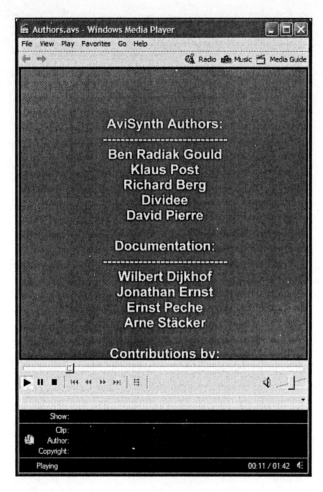

Check each of the sample scripts in the AviSynth subfolder by running them one at a time. Check the contents of the scripts by opening them with Notepad, and watch what plays in Windows Media Player. None of them uses a video source file.

Your working scripts don't need to go into the example folder. Store them in whatever folder(s) work best for you. Whenever you open a script, it will automatically call on the

AviSynth DLL engine, which will feed the frames to your default player, or the video software you open the script in.

Filters

As with VirtualDub, there are filters you can use in your AviSynth scripts. See `http://www.avisynth.org/`.

Desktop Icons and Your Default Player

You have installed the three software packages. There are just a couple things to do before finishing this chapter. Put icons on your desktop, and re-associate the AVS scripts to open with your preferred video player.

In your file manager, go to the executable files for VirtualDub, the AuxSetup one in the VirtualDub folder (the utility to test your hard drive), and VDubMod. Right-click on each of the executables and choose Send To | Desktop (create shortcut). You'll have icons on your desktop.

The AuxSetup hard drive test utility with VDubMod is the same one included with VirtualDub. There's no need to have two icons for the same utility on your desktop, so skip that one.

Windows XP has two versions of the Windows Media Player in the `c:\Program Files\Windows Media Player` folder: the latest one named `wmplayer.exe`, and a version 6.4 player named `mplayer2.exe`. If opening an AVS script file results in the version 6.4 player opening, and you prefer WMP9 or 10 (or another player), right-click on an AVS script in your browser, select Open With | Choose the program and check the option to always open files of that type with it.

Summary

You've seen a few samples of things you can do with VirtualDub, VDubMod, and AviSynth. You've installed the software, and you're ready to explore them further.

You may have noticed that some things were not mentioned in this introduction, such as the `aviproxy` subfolder of VirtualDub and its contents. These will be explained in a later chapter. Here we introduced you to the basics.

The rest of the book will help you use VirtualDub to implement your creative ideas with your video footage, as you explore the world of VirtualDub experientially.

The world of VirtualDub is forever spinning and you're in it, so hold on and enjoy the ride. Things can only get better.

2

Video Capture Equipment

Before I start talking about capturing equipment, I would like to draw your attention to various video-saving media. These media can be divided into analog and digital resources. Various magnetic tapes, including VHS and Hi8, are examples of analog-storing media. In these resources audio and video data are stored in the form of magnetic fields on a ribbon or positive film. Their quality will degrade with time and we need to **digitize** them in order to prevent losing video quality.

Digitizing is the process of capturing movie data from an analog source (like old movie media or a TV channel/ satellite receiver), converting it to a series of zeros and ones, and finally saving this on a digital media like CD or DVD.

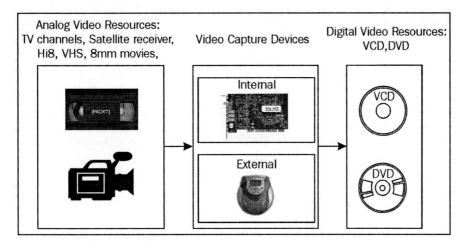

Other than maintenance of movie quality, is there any advantage for capturing analog movies? Yes. Consider the size of a VHS cassette and compare it with a CD or DVD. Can you imagine the space required for you to archive 100 movies as VHS? Now imagine the required space in the form of CDs.

Another subject is compatibility and support of media by players. Looking at your computer, you will see a CD or DVD drive. Stand-alone CD or DVD players are conventional player systems, which are found everywhere nowadays. On the other hand, players that support 8mm or Hi8 movies are not common.

Capturing video from an analog resource and saving it on a digital media has the following advantages:

- **Quality maintenance**: Zeros and ones are always zeros and ones and time can never destroy them.
- **Reduce media size**: CDs and DVDS are definitely smaller than 8mm or VHS cassettes.
- **Compatibility**: Almost everyone has a stand-alone VCD/DVD/CD player installed on his/her computer. However, most people do not have the equipment for playing an 8mm movie.

In this chapter, we will explore different aspects of the capturing process and the equipment required for this task. The subjects we will study deal with:

- **Analog video equipment**
- **Digital video resource**: DV, streaming video, VCD, DVD
- **Video capturing devices**: Internal capture cards, external receivers and converters, DV devices
- **Input/Output standards**: Composite Video, S Video, Antenna, FireWire
- **Equipment**: What you have to buy and why
- **Installing new hardware**
- **Tips for optimizing the capture process**

There are many devices for capturing video. They vary in price and functionality (from cheap TV tuner cards to expensive DV stations). A detailed discussion about each of these would require a separate book. Therefore, in this chapter, after introducing some basic requirements for capturing video, we will concentrate on a simple internal capture card that works fine with VirtualDub.

Analog Video Resources

Data is sent in the form of analog signals from an analog video resource. For example, TV broadcasting stations and satellite broadcasting TV channels are analog resources that send video and audio signals as electromagnetic waves. A VHS cassette player is another example of an analog resource that outputs analog video and audio signals.

We can categorize analog video resources into equipment that receives analog signals as waves (like a TV antenna or satellite receiver) and equipment that uses analog media (like 8mm, VHS, and Hi8 tapes). Various devices like **VCRs (Video Cassette Recorders**), Camcorders, and 8mm Projectors are needed to play these media.

We can get output signals from analog video resources using three output cables. (In fact we can find three input ports in every capture card used for receiving analog signals.)

The first port is the **antenna jack,** used for receiving analog signals from TV channels and satellite receivers. This port is used to capture video directly from the antenna:

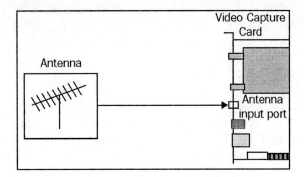

Alternatively, connect the antenna plug to the TV antenna jack and then connect the TV Composite video output port to the capture card Composite Video input port:

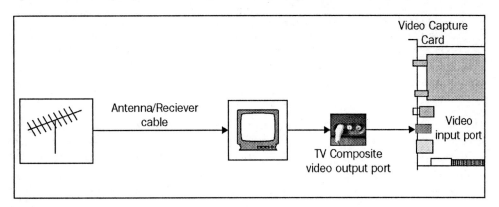

It is highly recommended that you do not use the antenna input of the capture card to capture from VCRs.

Composite Video is another standard port that is widely used in various video players. You can find this output in almost every VHS player and Hi8 camcorder.

The last output standard in video players and camcorders having good quality is the **S-Video port:**

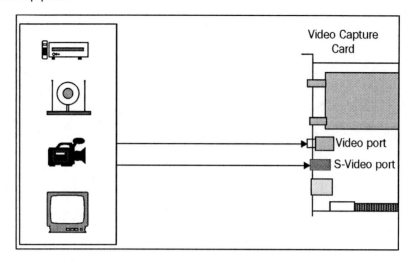

Since S-Video is a predefined standard, we don't need to do much work on tuning VirtualDub channels for receiving signals if we use this port to connect the capture card to the video resource.

Digital Video Resources

The two major types of digital resources are DV and Streaming video.

We have not categorized VCDs and DVDs as digital resources because our topic of discussion is capturing. We seldom use VirtualDub to capture videos from a VCD or a DVD and make copies of them, unless we do not have a CD or DVD player installed on our computer.

Sometimes processing video on a VCD or DVD may become necessary. For example, we may need to cut a section of movie from a VCD, add some subtitles and effects to it, and save it as a new VCD. In these situations, even though we do not capture the input video from digital media but simply open a file with VirtualDub, we are still dealing with a digital resource.

DV stands for **Digital Video,** which has become a popular standard in recent years. With this format, we can convert analog signals to digital ones at the hardware level. This task provides high quality at considerable speed. Therefore, the capture card is no longer necessary. All we need is a port named **FireWire** to connect the DV equipment (including DV camcorders or other external/internal DV devices) to the computer:

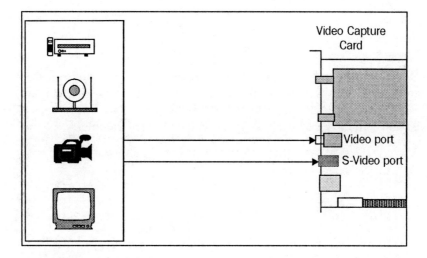

FireWire is rightly promoted as having a bandwidth of 400 megabits per second; however, the digital video being transferred from the camcorder uses very little of this bandwidth and video capturing is still done in real-time.

What is the role of VirtualDub in a scenario where a device with the DV feature can convert and compress the analog inputs to digital outputs in a piece of hardware? With the help of DV, we may obtain a direct compressed file from an analog resource, but what about personal processing (like inserting subtitles) using artistic filters? VirtualDub can receive input from DV devices, so we will discuss them in this chapter.

The Nature of DV (Digital Video)

This section points out some features of DV and will give you a clear idea about this subject:

- **DV is a new format**: DV is the name of a single video format compression used for compressing raw video data. It is, however, not the name of a category encompassing *all* digital formats. For example, an MPEG file is not a DV. A DV data stream can be saved as an AVI, but an AVI file is not a DV. An AVI is just a container format that can hold many video formats.

- **DV is not related to DVD and VCD**: A DVD is not a DV. A DVD is a disc type and a playback format. In a DVD, MPEG files and audio files are mixed into VOB files. A DV on the other hand is a single format of video compression. In the same way, a VCD is not a DV. DV is simply a digital format for storing video.

- **DV cannot be 'captured'**: Files can be *converted* and *transferred* into digital format with the help of the DV standard. The term 'capture' refers to the re-acquisition of motion images in a format that is different from the analog source format. In the DV equipment, compression occurs in an IC and then the compressed information is transferred from device X to device Y (using special wires and ports—called FireWire or IEEE1394).

- **DV cannot be called a special cable or port**: DV is the name of the video compression format that is produced with the help of special equipment. Standard wires and ports called IEEE1394 or FireWire (or iLink, as Sony named it) help transfer the compressed data to the computer:

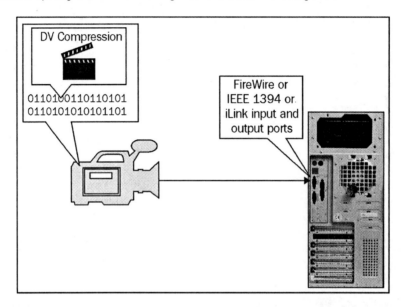

- **DV is not a measure of capture card functionality**: You cannot consider a video capture card without a FireWire port and cable as a poor device because video capture capability is not related to the FireWire port. It is strongly recommended that you do not buy capture cards with FireWire ports (merely IEEE1394 ports) installed on them. As seen with the ATI All in Wonder 8500DV, the *DV* aspect of the card may have caused problems. If you search on the Internet, you will see many hardware conflicts and errors reported. If you want to work with the DV standard, buy a high-quality dedicated FireWire card.

- **DV-based capture equipment**: DV capture devices can be categorized into internal and external hardware. With such equipment we can receive video signals from an analog resource and then convert them to DV data. The DV data is then fed to the computer. Either the computer can accept this raw DV data via the DV transfer software, or the user can use a software-capturing solution to convert it to another format on the fly. Due to DV functionality, some users stay away from the latter. In most internal computer capture cards, users are able to select a desired format for captured video whereas the DV capture devices can only perform hardware-capture in DV format. The user will not be able to software-capture the transferred data later. Once compression takes place, it cannot be undone and stays permanent.

Streaming Video

Streaming video is another kind of digital video resource mainly used in cyberspace communications. Internet TV channels and teleconferences are samples of online streaming video. The main difference between a streaming video file (like RealVideo or streamed WMV) and other video files is that we can play a streaming file while downloading it from the internet even when we are in the middle of the download process. In fact the playback task begins when the player buffer (e.g. Windows Media Player buffer) has collected enough video information. For streaming video, we just save the data after the download has been completed. We do not need a capture card for this purpose. With the help of certain software applications, we can store streamed video on our hard disk:

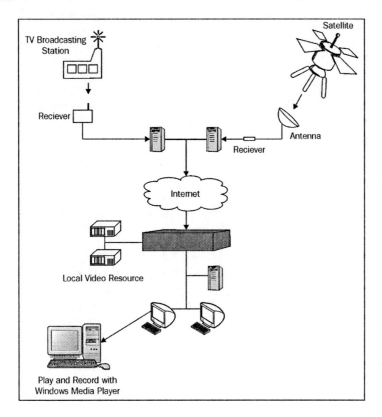

Different Types of Capturing Devices

We can divide capturing devices into two main groups: internal devices and external devices. Internal devices need to be installed on an empty PCI slot on the motherboard. We can categorize them as:

1. **TV tuners with composite and/or S-Video input**: They are cheaper and function better than professional capture cards. Pinnacle PCTV, V-Stream PCI TV-PVR Tuner, and Hauppauge PVR250 TV Tuner Card are examples of such capture cards.

2. **Graphics card with integrated video capture chip**: Such cards have some extra input ports for receiving analog signals (such as ATI All-in-Wonder).

3. **FireWire (IEEE1394/iLink) cards**: These cards are usually used for digital video capture. These devices have an internal chip for video compression and the captured data is provided using the DV format.

> DS PYRO Professional is one of the perfect and the world's best-selling 1394/FireWire cards. Adobe Premiere Pro software is included with this device. Other samples of FireWire cards include: Mercury FireWire PCI card (3 external FireWire ports and 1 internal FireWire port), D-LINK 1394 (3 FireWire Ports w 2 USB Ports), and ATI All In One Combo (3 FireWire Ports w 2 USB Ports).

4. **Professional capture cards supporting every standard video port and featuring real-time video encoding and decoding**: ATI All-In-Wonder RADEON 9700 PRO 8X and Pinnacle DC1000 are examples of such video capture devices.

It's hard to classify items of external capturing equipment because the input/output ports differ across different equipment. Besides, they vary in functionality. Some of them act just as a terminal, some compress internally, and others act as receivers besides capturing video. For most of them, the output ports for the PC are FireWire and/or USB.

However, there are exceptions. For example, Pinnacle Studio MP10 External Video Capture connects to the PC's parallel port. However, there are a lot of problems with the supplied software as well as with the drivers. If you get it working, you'll find that the audio doesn't sync up with the video and there are many lost video frames in the captured clip. You'll find all such problems documented on the MP10 forums at http://www.pinnaclesys.com/.

The cost of external capture devices varies based on various features, including the quality. For example, Pyro AV Link API-550 (made by ADS Technologies) costs approximately $250 and captures well from digital resources. However, it will skip some frames randomly while capturing from an analog video source such as a VHS or VCR.

Pinnacle Dazzle DVC120 (USB1/2) is another great external device that quickly and easily connects any video device (including analogue and digital camcorders or VCRs) to any PC—even PCs with poor hardware.

This device encodes video in DVD quality and transfers it to any computer via a standard USB port. It can produce the following formats for captured data based on our choice:

- Video CD (VCD) or Super Video CD (SVCD) with an optional CD-R or CD-RW drive
- DVD with an optional DVD-R DVD-RW or DVD+RW drive
- MPEG-1 & MPEG-2
- AVI
- RealVideo 8
- Windows Media Format, including Windows Media 9

Canopus ADVC300 ($499.00) is the ultimate bi-directional analog to digital video converter unit for the video enthusiast. Besides capturing video from various video resources, this device features high quality image-enhancement technology including digital noise reduction.

Internal versus External Equipment

What are the advantages and disadvantages of internal and external capturing equipment? Let us summarize from the previous sections:

- **More control of compression format**: We use internal capturing cards when the video compression scheme needs to be set manually. Since most external equipment uses DV format, we usually cannot set the target captured file type.

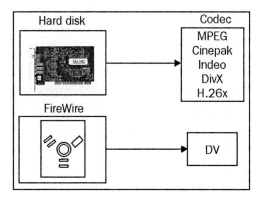

- **Heavy processing with minimum system resources**: If we have a slow computer with low storage space, we use external capturing devices. Capturing with internal cards eats up a huge chunk of system resources and needs a fast CPU and enormous hard space. External capturing devices do not capture and compress inside the computer. So even with a slow machine we can capture our analog videos. In this situation, the only thing we need is a FireWire port installed on the computer.

- **No PCI slot available**: If other cards have filled all PCI slots in our computer, we should use external video capturing equipment. Also, in laptops we normally have to use an external device for capturing.

- **Money matters**: Usually internal capture cards are cheaper than external devices (please keep in mind this is not true for professional internal capture cards). So if money is a constraint, we can choose internal capture cards.

- **Quality and capture facility**: While comparing captured video from internal and external equipment, we may find that the internal capture card does not faithfully reproduce the color and/or motion of the original video. Most people will agree that external devices do the capturing and compressing processes faster, more easily, and produce better quality than internal video capture cards.

What to Buy

We now understand what analog/digital video resources are and what internal and external video capture devices are. So which capture card should we buy, how much money must we pay for it, and how can we use it?

Although VirtualDub can receive video information from almost any capturing equipment, we will concentrate on internal capturing cards since we are going to study VirtualDub processing features together (including various codecs).

If you are new to the world of video capturing, start with a suitably priced internal device with acceptable functionality. I recommend a Pinnacle PCTV capture card. It has a low price, has been on the market for considerable time, and is not buggy.

I am not the marketing manager of any video capture card manufacturer! What I will tell you about capture cards is based on my personal experiments. Please keep in mind that even if a video capture card does not work for me, it may be suitable for you. Beside the capture card performance, other things directly affect its functionality.

For example, on visiting the ATI website you'll see that guys who bought ATI TV Wonder card had many problems in capturing, unless their video card was an ATI-supported video card (such as any ATI, 3Dfx Banshee, or S3 Savage 3D). Before buying a new capture card, you should request product details and technical information from the manufacturer's website. Look for any compatibility issues in hardware discussion forums and sites. There are many of them on the Internet, for example:

```
http://www.electronics-reviews-now.com/Video/index.html
```

Other than an internal capture card (Pinnacle PCTV for example), there are some other requirements such as:

- **System resources**: Capturing is a resource-consuming process, so your computer must be powerful to achieve good results. For capturing and processing video signals the Celeron 333 MHz with 128 MB and 20 GB hard space used for Office Applications (Word, Excel, and Access etc.) would probably be insufficient. A Pentium IV 2.4 GHz or higher would be suitable for this task. Keep in mind that after capturing video, you will have a huge primary video file that should be saved on the hard disc for further processing. An 80 GB hard disk would be helpful at the beginning although a 120 GB one is preferable.

- **Recording equipment**: After capturing and processing video data, we need to store them on digital media (like CD and DVD). So we need a DVD R/W or CD R/W installed on our system to make a VCD or DVD from our captured video.

Installing Capturing Equipment

Installing external capturing devices is fairly simple. Just connect the input and output ports with the required cables, turn on the computer and video resource, and start capturing. For example, to watch TV on your computer using the WinTV-USB equipment, just plug the USB port into the computer and the device will be at your service. WinTV-USB allows you to:

- Watch or record videos from a VCR, camcorder, or DVD player through the auxiliary audio/video input (S-Video or composite)
- Hold videoconferences over the Internet
- Snap still video images in JPEG, BMP, etc. formats
- Make video movies in AVI file format
- Receive teletext pages (European models)
- Listen to FM radio while you work on your PC (WinTV-USB-FM models)

However, you need to install internal cards on your motherboard physically. This process is not too hard and if you can work with a screwdriver then you can install your internal capturing device. The step-by-step installation process is given below:

1. Turn off your computer and disconnect it from the power supply.

2. Loosen the computer's cover screws and remove the case shield.

3. By touching the outside of the case body, discharge yourself of static electricity since it may damage the board.

4. Find a free PCI slot and remove the slot's cover at the back of the case. (Keep the screw. You will need it very soon.)

5. Connect the internal connector of the capture card to the sound card. There is no need to insert an external sound card jack to the output sound port.

6. Now insert the card on the PCI slot and push it gently onto the motherboard at both ends of card.

7. If the card does not fit easily, pull it out and try one more time. Do *not* press it to the motherboard until it bends or else you may break some internal circuits and wreck your system.

Manufacturers describe this task in the printed manual of the product and help files are included in the companion CD too.

Every internal capture card comes with a device driver that should be installed after installing the board. Turn on your computer and after a while the Add New Hardware Wizard dialog will appear. Insert the driver CD and click on Next.

Do not change anything in the next window and press Next one more time. After a little delay, the path and the target driver files will be detected from the CD and the installation process will start automatically.

At the end of the installation press Finish and restart Windows. Your capture card will be presented in the Device manager list and will be ready for use.

Connecting Video Resources to the Capture Card

Let us study the input and output ports of a Pinnacle PCTV card. As already seen in the figures in the *Analogue Video Resources* section in this chapter, we have three input ports and one output audio port. The first port is an antenna input. Use this for capturing from TV channels. Just plug the antenna jack into this port and then in VirtualDub select the target input for video as TV tuner (the complete description of this process will be provided in the next chapter). After fine-tuning the channels, you should be able to see your desired channel at the preview area in VirtualDub and can then start the capturing process by pressing *F6* or *F5*.

Below this port, there is an output port for audio. We can connect speakers to this port to hear received signals:

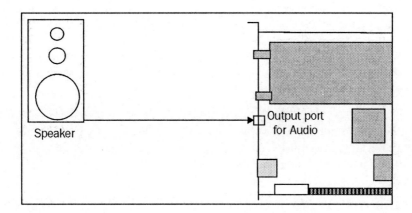

If you connect the video capture card to the sound card internally, there is no need to plug the speaker jack into this port:

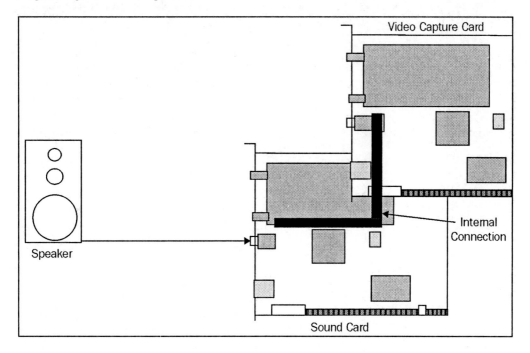

The next port is a Composite Video port that can be used for capturing video from **VTR** (Video Tape Recorder), satellite receiver, camcorder, and TV tuner. As usual, just plug the video resource composite video jack into this port and fine-tune inside VirtualDub.

If your video source has an S-Video output, then use this one instead of any other video capture card inputs because the quality of an S-Video port is higher than other ports.

For example, you can connect a VTR to the capture card through the antenna or the composite video socket. If you decide to use the antenna socket, you need to tune your PCTV card to channel 36 or 23 (or something else, based on your country). Nevertheless, even if you tune your card perfectly, you will never get the same quality as if you were using a composite or S-Video input.

There will be even more incompatibility issues if the VTR and the capture card were made for different countries with different video standards! For example, you would have trouble with the sound if your PCTV card was made for the UK, while your VTR came from Japan and you were using the antenna input.

Final Tips and Optimizations for Better Video Capture

Ready to capture? Before capturing let me show you some system optimizations that may lead to better quality in captured video. We need these optimizations because we are dealing with a large amount of data during capture. If our system is not optimized enough we may lose some frames and the resulting clip will look jerky.

Let's start with hard disk optimization. Regardless of whether you use an entire hard disk or a specific partition for capturing, it is important that before starting the capture process, you format that drive with the Full option and not with the Quick option. Quick formatting just marks old files on the hard surface as 'erased' and the real data remains on the disk. This issue will affect the storing of captured video data because for saving them, the old data must be erased permanently and this task wastes some processing capacity.

Another tip is to defragment the capturing partition. Saving and deleting files on a partition may allow some gaps to remain on the disk surface. The hard disk will fill these gaps when saving new captured data. This increases access time and you may lose some frames. However, with a defragmented partition, data will be saved contiguously. You can use any system utility or Windows defragmenting program for this task:

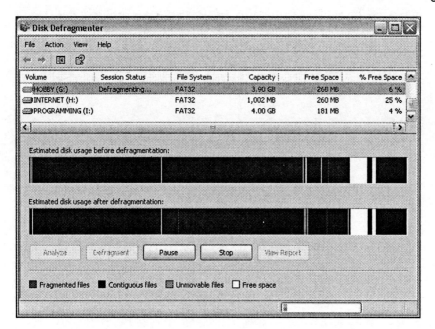

Another group of optimizations deals with the CPU. For better performance during capture, unload and disable any unnecessary programs and Windows activities including screen savers because they may get activated in the middle of capturing and interfere with the process.

Unload any unnecessary applications. Press *Ctrl+Alt+Del* to activate the Task Manager dialog. Select the application and press the End Task button:

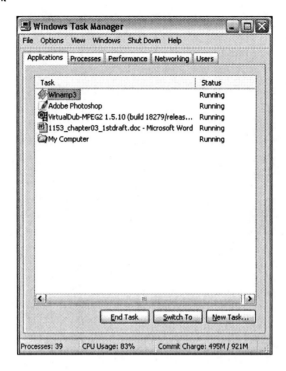

Turn off any unnecessary peripherals including printers and scanners. Disable the network card because sending or receiving data over the network can affect the capture process.

Install your capture card in the first PCI slot (slot zero) if possible. Slots are checked based on their number priority.

Make sure that the CPU and motherboard temperatures are under control. Sometimes capturing looks good at the beginning, but the number of dropped frames increases in the next few hours. If this is the case, then you should check the case and CPU fans.

Summary

In this chapter we learned that there are two sources for video: analog and digital. We also learned that the capturing equipment can be divided into internal and external devices. Generally, external devices are expensive and powerful because capture and compression tasks take place at the hardware level. These, however, allow less control over the format of the captured video. Internal capture cards are usually cheaper and exercise more control on the video format since some application like VirtualDub is used for capturing and compressing captured video. Finally we discovered that we can do some hard disk and Windows optimizations to decrease dropped frames during capturing and get a smooth video.

3
Capture Preprocessing

It is time to make some software settings for the actual capturing process, assuming we have set up all the equipment in the right order from the previous chapter. These settings include file, video, audio, and capture settings inside VirtualDub, and are necessary to get an appropriate video file. The following diagram is a graphical representation of the capture preprocessing workflow:

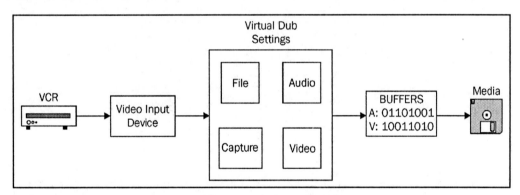

We will study all these configurations step by step, in this chapter. Moreover, we will consider a practical example in which the entire capturing process, from receiving input analog signals to preparing them for writing in a popular DVD format, will be illustrated.

By the end of this chapter, we'll be able to:

- Select a suitable approach (VFW or WDM) for the capturing process, based on your Windows version
- Specify file settings including: Name, Path, Allocated space
- Define suitable timing and disk I/O for a capturing process
- Achieve multisegment capturing
- Set the audio compression and volume
- Set the video characteristics: frame size, frame rate, color depth

- Set the video standard for capturing
- Set the desirable format and compression for captured data
- Define suitable buffer size and number
- Save capture settings for future use

Defining an Input Source for VirtualDub

We want to connect VirtualDub to the source so that it will receive the captured data. To do this, we can use the companion application that came with the capturing card, enable the input channel that we want to capture, and close the application.

Run VirtualDub and select File | Capture avi. Another alternative is to open the Video Source window by pressing S in the Capture mode window (or selecting Video | Source from this window) and, in the Select a Video Source drop-down list, choose the desired input source. There are a number of input sources for video, which may vary based on the capturing card:

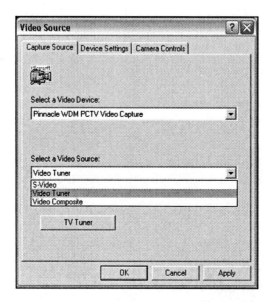

Choose the TV input source (i.e. Video Tuner), and click on TV Tuner in this dialog box. In the next dialog (assuming you've set the correct options while installing the new capture card), leave the settings unchanged, and just enter the number of the desired channel in the Channel group. Now, press *Enter*.

If no channels have been detected yet, it's possible to find them automatically by pressing the AutoTune button.

After pressing AutoTune, the channel number, and Video and Audio frequencies change rapidly to find a channel:

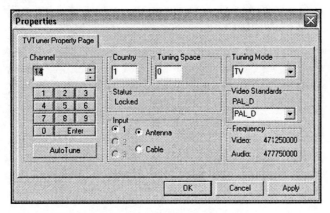

Press OK to close the above dialog box. If all cable connections and channel settings are correct, the desired image will be shown in the preview area.

In the right area of the following screenshot, there is some data about the current job. These fields will show some statistical information during the capturing process:

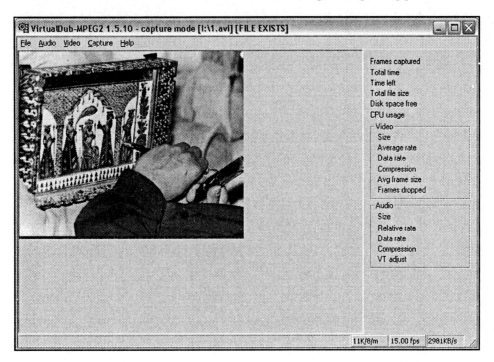

At the bottom of the above screenshot is the status bar, which shows capturing events and three buttons for video and audio settings. VirtualDub computes the required space for storing captured data per second, depending on the quality we set for video and audio, and shows the results in the next field.

Now that we have input signals from an analog resource, it's time to make other settings inside VirtualDub required to achieve digital data. These settings can be divided into four categories: **File settings**, **Audio settings**, **Video Settings**, and **Capture settings**.

File Settings

File settings in VirtualDub include defining the name and path, and allocating space for storing capturing data. All these settings can be done from the File menu:

By default, the first captured data is stored with the name of capture.avi in the My Documents\Captured Files\Videos\ folder:

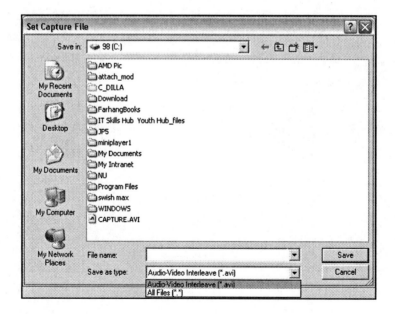

However, we can set our favorite name and path by using the File | Set capture file option (or pressing *F2*). We can define the desired settings in the window that appears, as illustrated above.

After defining the base file name, every time we capture analogue signals, a counter increments the number of the file name and prepares it for the next capture.

For example, suppose we set the file name `sample.avi` at the root directory of `c:\`. After the first capture if we try to capture data one more time, the number 1 will be added to the file name (i.e. `c:\capture1.avi`); for the next capture 2 will be added (i.e. `c:\capture2.avi`), and so on.

Regardless of what number we use for file names, in the next capture, that number will be automatically incremented.

For example, if you set `44.avi` as the first file name, the next file will be captured with the name `45.avi`.

There are two options in the File menu to go back and forth in the existing and unused file IDs. These are File | Previous file ID and File | Next file ID.

If the file already exists, an alerting tag will be shown in the title bar of the capturing window:

VirtualDub-MPEG2 1.5.10 - capture mode [I:\1.avi] [FILE EXISTS]

Audio Settings

There are three options in the Audio menu for receiving audio signals from the capture card, setting sound volume and channel balance, and the sound compression scheme:

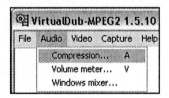

If the captured signals are without sound, then we must check out the internal Windows mixer to make sure Line in is selected as the audio source.

Selecting the Audio | Windows mixer option will show the mixer, in which the audio input source can be set:

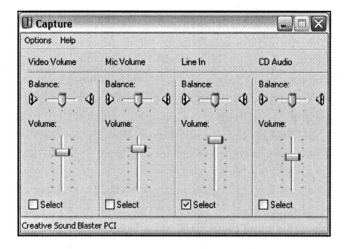

In the Volume meter dialog box, we should see one of following images, depending upon whether we have stereo or mono settings. We can use the VUMeter, Oscilloscope, and Analyzer radio buttons for changing sound balance, volumes, and the graphical representation of audio signals:

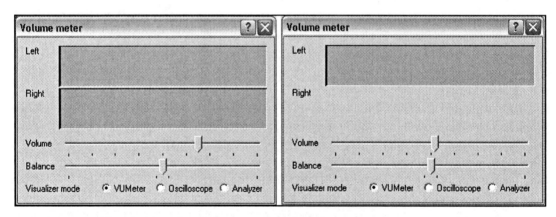

We can set stereo or mono sound at the bottom of the VirtualDub window. Just click on this button and hold the mouse button for a while. From the following list, we can choose our desired sound settings for capturing. For the example given above (capturing for DVD), we need to select 44.10 KHz, 16-bit, stereo, as shown in the following window:

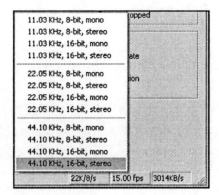

In the context of multimedia, a huge amount of space is required to save uncompressed data. Therefore, we must use some compression algorithms to reduce the file size. In VirtualDub, all audio characteristics, including format and capturing quality, can be found under the Audio | Compression option. Please note that in this dialog box the format is different from the codec that will be used later for saving the captured data.

If you do not want to be concerned with audio details, and just want a good audio scheme, select CD Quality from the Name drop-down list.

The Format section defines how to arrange audio signals in a file and the Attributes section sets the basic sound quality:

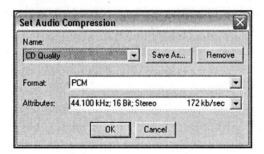

If we define custom settings in this dialog box, we can use the Save As button to save it with our desired name. For future usages, we can just select that setting from the Name drop-down list. We can delete that scheme from the list by pressing the Remove button.

Video Settings

The Video menu provides many more options than the Audio menu. Some of these options are used for visualization in VirtualDub capture mode, and some of them are used for video capture settings:

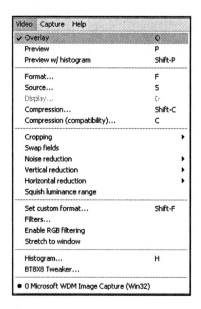

The first step in the video settings is defining the video format. Press *F* (or choose Video | Format) to activate the Video Format dialog box. There are two drop-down lists that we can use for setting the frame size and pixel format.

A box next to these two fields shows the size of each uncompressed frame, based on the selected options. For example, if we select 320x240 for Resolution and RGB 555 (16 bit) for Pixel Depth, then the size of each frame can be computed as:

320 (pixels) x 240 (pixels) x 2 (bytes or 16bit) = 153600

This field is designed to give an overall idea about the size of the captured video:

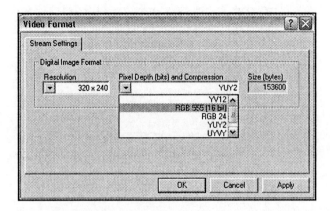

Select YUY2, since we have decided to capture data for a DVD. We can then choose the MPEG 4 codec later. After setting frame size and pixel format, press Apply, and then OK to close this window.

Look at the current captured image in the preview area. Some color and light corrections maybe necessary, depending upon what channel or input source signals we receive:

Press *S* one more time (Video | Source), and in the Video Source dialog box, go to the Device Settings tab. All sliders in this area are self-explanatory and the changes can be seen while tuning them in the preview area. Pressing the Default button will return all sliders to their original position:

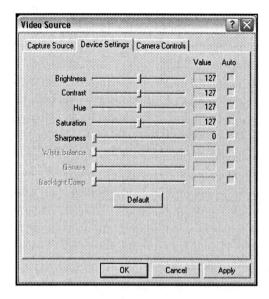

Press Apply, and OK after you achieve the desired settings:

Compressing Input Signals while Capturing

We can compress input signals while capturing. There are various options in the Video |
Compression (*Shift+C*) window, based on what format we choose for video.

For example, if we select RGB for pixels format, the following compression codecs will
be available:

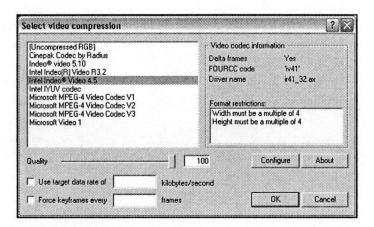

Remember that it's possible to add some additional codecs to Windows. So the new codecs will be shown in the compression windows if the pixel format (color space) can support them.

Additional codecs like Huffyuv and MJPEG can be downloaded from the following sites:

Huffyuv:

http://neuron2.net/www.math.berkeley.edu/benrg/huffyuv.html

http://www.free-codecs.com/download/HuffYUV.htm

MJPEG:

http://www.morgan-multimedia.com/

http://www.free-codecs.com/download/Motion_JPEG_Codec.htm

Every codec in the window has some options that can be used for size and compression settings. There is one global rule for almost every codec setting: increasing the quality results in increasing the file size.

You may wonder why there are two Video | Compression options in VirtualDub: one in the main VirtualDub window (*Ctrl+P*), and one in the VirtualDub capture mode (*Shift+C*).

This is because the end codecs tend to be too slow to be used on slow computers in real-time. So we use fast codecs to capture data signals, and slow codecs (that can compress better than fast codecs) to do the final encoding.

For our DVD example, choose Microsoft MPEG-4 Video Codec V3 from the list. Then press the Configure button and set the sliders, as shown in the following screenshot:

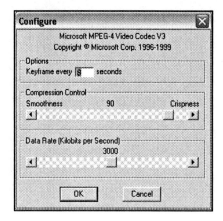

Cropping Videos

We can crop the video during the capture process. Click on Video | Cropping | Enable, and then select Video | Cropping | Set bounds. In the following screenshot, X1 and X2 set the left and right margins and Y1 and Y2 set the up and down margins respectively:

Some frames may drop because cropping during capture needs heavy processing. Therefore, it is strongly recommended that you use cropping after capturing video, or use small values for cropping.

Removing Unwanted Noises from Videos

Another technique for video optimization is reducing the noise. This can be enabled by selecting Video | Noise reduction | Enabled:

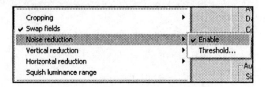

We can set the noise threshold with the slider that appears after selecting Video | Noise reduction | Threshold.

Reducing File Size

There are two options for horizontal and vertical reduction. This feature is useful for powerful capture cards capable of getting signals at high resolution. A good capture card is not enough, and we need a powerful CPU too, or we may lose some frames during the reduction process.

Vertical and horizontal reduction options can be found in the Video menu. For better quality use the 2:1 Cubic option:

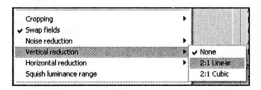

For more compression, use the 2:1 Linear option:

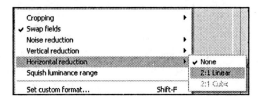

Unusual Resolutions and Formats

For authoring standard VCDs, SVCDs, and DVDs it's better to use standard PAL, or NTSC settings. However, in some situations, if you prefer to use different resolutions and pixel formats you can refer to Video | Set custom format and select the resolution and data format that you wish.

If your preferred resolution does not exist in the frame size group, check the Use custom size box, and insert the desired resolution manually. Not every resolution is allowed. For example, if you enter a resolution in which the video width is less than its height, the following error message box will appear:

When you decide to use custom format, it's preferable to use a low resolution and YUV family data format as illustrated below. The number of dropped frames is consequently reduced and the video will have reasonable quality:

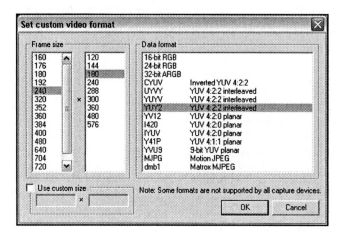

Histogram

The **histogram** option provides a graphical representation of the colors in the current frame. With this ability, we can study the color structure of input signals during capture and make any necessary changes. Activate this feature through Video | Histogram:

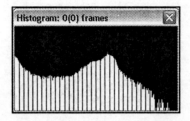

Use histogram only if your CPU is powerful enough. Otherwise, you may lose some frames during capture.

Capture Settings

All options we need for capturing (from configuration to starting the real job) lie in the Capture menu. Pressing *F6* (Capture | Capture video) or *F5* (compatibility mode) starts the actual video capturing.

Before doing this, however, we need to do some configuration in the Capture menu:

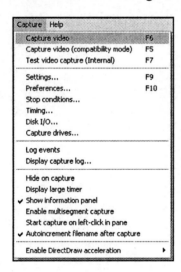

Press *F9* (or choose Capture | Settings) to activate the Capture Settings window. For standard videos (PAL and NTSC), we should set different values in this window. For example, in order to capture for the PAL system we should use the following settings:

There are four controls in the Capture options group. Selecting Capture audio saves audio signals too, and activating Wait for OK to capture will show a message box like the one above, after pressing *F5* or *F6*. For continuing capture, we press OK.

For NTSC, the suitable settings are:

The most important control in this group is Frame rate, which is used to set the video capturing frame rate. It is possible to define frame rates with up to four digits after decimal point. We used this feature for setting NTSC standard. NTSC has 29.97 frame rates, but because of an internal issue in VirtualDub, we must use 29.9697, for NTSC.

The last control in this group is a button that can be used for computing the frame rate, nearest to the current number.

In the Abort options group we can choose the keys and mouse buttons that can abort the capturing process. Selecting Escape and Space will abort capturing if one of these keys is pressed. We can also choose the left and right mouse buttons for this purpose.

The Advanced group includes some serious controls for capturing. The percentage of frames that are allowed to be dropped during capture is set in the Drop % limit field.

The Buffer

A **buffer** is a piece of memory that is used to temporarily hold data while waiting for the hard disk. The number of buffers is limited by available free disk space. Although it's possible to use up to 10 audio buffers, it's better to use a 10 video buffers and 4 audio buffers combination.

In the Audio buffer size field, we can set the required space for gathering audio signals in bytes. If you specify a small size for this field, CPU load will increase noticeably—and you will lose some frames, as a result. Setting a big value for this field will show lack of video synchronization.

Saving Current Configurations for Future Reference

Pressing *F10* (Capture | Preferences) will show the following window, in which we can set the capturing preferences. If you plan to use a special path and file name for capturing, then type it in the Default capture file field.

For saving current capture, audio, and video settings check the Save current capture, Save current audio, and Save current video boxes respectively.

Leave the other controls unchanged because we've set them in previous menus:

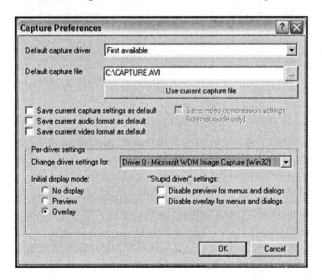

How can we tell VirtualDub to stop capturing, if unwanted situations occur?

Capture | Stop conditions shows us a window for defining capturing stop conditions:

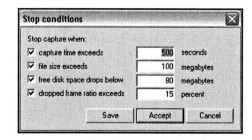

The Synchronization Problem

Sometimes in the capturing process, video, and audio don't match correctly. There are many reasons for this, including: unusual video frame rates, weak processors, and background activities during running VirtualDub.

With the Capture | Timing option we can solve this problem. We can resample audio during capture to match the video frame rate by selecting the last option of this window. By selecting this option, we can ignore dropped frames:

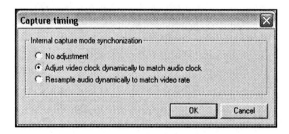

Chunks

Chunks are synchronized video and audio packages that sit in the buffer before they are written on the disk. Through Capture | Disk I/O we can set the size and number of chunks in each buffer.

The size of each resultant buffer (based on chunk size and number settings) is a very important factor for suitable capturing. If we select buffers that are too small, we will get too much file I/O and data will be synchronized correctly, but the CPU load and HDD activities will increase, and VirtualDub may drop some frames. If we select buffers that are too large, the synchronization will be affected.

After testing various settings, try to balance these factors based on the hardware that you have, to get the optimized result.

In fact, we must use this section for matching VirtualDub with the speed of the computer. It's recommended that you use 1MB chunk size, and 14 chunks for disks with at least 2MB cache, and a 1GHz CPU.

At the bottom of this window, we can see that the Disable Windows write buffering option has been checked. This prevents any disk management application (and Windows, itself) from interfering:

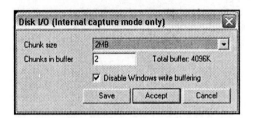

Capture Duration Restrictions

Is there any restriction for capturing duration? Yes, there is. In fact, the only restriction for file size is the disk space.In VirtualDub, we can capture AVI files with more than 2 GB! There is an ability called Spill System (Capture | Capture Drives), which can be used for dividing large files into several parts. VirtualDub will see these parts as one logical file in the next call.

In Spill System Setup we can specify the partitions of captured data:

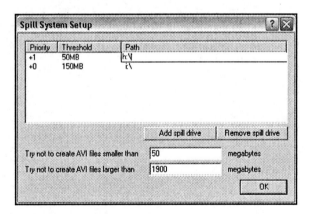

Defining more than one spill drive is allowed. However, this is not the whole story. For activating spill drives that we've defined, we should enable the multi-segment capture feature. Just check the corresponding option: Video | Enable Multisegment capture.

If you think every thing is alright, press *F6* to start the capturing process. The right pane of the window shows some statistical information. This area indicates how many frames have been captured, how much of CPU capacity used, how many frames dropped, etc:

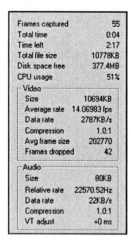

If you wish to see a larger counter during capture, select Capture | Display Larger Timer.

Keep watching, and if you find that the CPU usage is more than 90%, you may notice that the value of dropped frames increases. Just review all your settings one more time and make any necessary changes (e.g. reduce capture resolution).

If you are using Win XP or 2K, activate the Capture | Enable DirectDraw Acceleration | Both fields option for better performance. Make sure that Video | Overlay is selected:

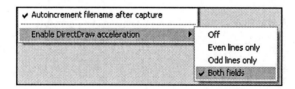

For Win9x and ME, deselecting this option will be useful for better performance. If your hardware is not powerful enough, deactivating Video | preview maybe helpful too.

Leave the computer alone during capture or at least don't ask it to do another heavy task!

To stop, just click the VirtualDub window, press the *ESCAPE* key, or use any other settings that you've made for stopping capture. The File | Exit capture mode takes us back to the VirtualDub main window.

Summary

We have been introduced to some capture preprocessing that is very important for creating optimized videos. We learned that VirtualDub configuration for capturing falls into four categories:

- File settings
- Audio Settings
- Video Settings
- Capture Settings

Moreover, we learned that before writing captured signals on disk they should be buffered for better disk I/O management and optimized data capturing. Also, with the help of some VirtualDub internal mechanisms called Spill System Setup and Multi Segment Capturing we can capture and save files with more than 2GB.

In the next chapter, we will learn how to use some filters to optimize captured data.

4

Processing with VirtualDub

So we have captured our video: what now? What can we do with it and even more importantly, why would we want to do that with VirtualDub? What facilities does VirtualDub offer that might suit our needs? This chapter will answer all those questions in detail and at the same time give you a brief tour of the VirtualDub interfaces.

What we often do not realize is how "raw" a piece of captured footage is. It is usually uncompressed or compressed at awfully low compression ratios and therefore takes up a lot of your hard-disk space. Storage has become very cheap nowadays but not cheap enough to archive movies in this form. Even playback is impaired on older machines since uncompressed video is computationally very demanding. But suppose you could archive and play it without problems, it is quite probable that your capture would not be perfect, no matter how good you are with a camcorder or how good the quality of your TV reception is. In the first case, there will be unwanted scenes, unbalanced colors, artifacts that were not visible when you viewed the video on your TV, and so on. In the second case, you might get noise, or commercials to interrupt the march of events right on their peak. Before I forget, let me mention that you can also use VirtualDub to process files you got from the Internet; you can even use it to fix that damaged file you recovered from an old CD!

In all honesty, although VirtualDub is not what the entertainment industry uses to edit the movies we watch on the big screen, it can fulfill the needs of an amateur. If you got excited with capturing the video onto your computer-disk, wait until you read the following chapters! VirtualDub compares very well against the typical commercial video-editing packages. Well, it's free to start with—meaning you will not have to spend a dime to get it or use it (if you haven't done so already, download it from http://www.virtualdub.org/). Additionally, commercial packages are specifically designed to meet the needs of professionals. These, however, seem complex and somewhat chaotic to someone who is just getting started. VirtualDub is very simple to use, (once you familiarize yourself with it) and at the same time very powerful—and that is a great combination. I personally do not think of VirtualDub as an application that I have to use because there is no alternative, but rather because it suits my needs well.

However, let's look at what you can do with VirtualDub: the possibilities are numerous:

- Remove the annoying commercials from a TV program you have captured
- Cut a segment of the same video and create a degraded snapshot video that you distribute on the Internet or a collection of favorite scenes of a show
- Adjust the dimensions of a video in both the spatial and temporal dimensions
- Add audio to a video or edit the existing audio
- Recover (partially or even in full) a damaged file
- Increase the perceived quality or change the playback speed of a video by altering the frame rate
- Remove artifacts introduced in videos originating from interlaced sources
- Adjust the color information
- Add an "age" effect by converting it to monochrome or black and white
- Remove logos that have been superimposed on the video
- Other effects that you might not have thought of before but will trigger your imagination as you read the following chapters

As you learn the steps through the practical examples that follow, you will be a lot more familiar with the concepts and techniques used. In the long term, you will be able to combine your creativity and imagination with what you have learned to make excellent use of the application.

VirtualDub Processing Functions

If you thought that what I said in the previous section was vague, thanks for your patience; I will get the chance to add the missing details in the following paragraphs. My aim in this section is to introduce the functionality that makes possible all the things I have mentioned previously. Let's take a look at the major functions one by one to see what they are useful for, and how they work internally.

Append, Cut, Copy, and Paste

If you have ever used any text-processing application, you must be familiar with Cut, Copy, and Paste—the three essential clipboard functions. The latter are replicated in VirtualDub, thus allowing you to quickly re-arrange portions of a video. Although the uses are obvious, here are a couple of examples in case nothing comes straight to mind:

- If you are compiling a sketch and a scene was shot out of order, you can then cut the scene, search to the required point in time and paste it.

- If you want to give emphasis on a particular event, you can copy and paste it at the end to simulate repetition.

Additionally, VirtualDub provides an append function that lets you append one video file at the end of another. This function is not very different from copy and paste: it only works on different files. The ordinary cut, copy, and paste functions will only work within the same file; more specifically, you cannot copy a portion of a video from one window of VirtualDub and paste it to another video in a different window, as you copy from Notepad with text.

Last but not least, the append function requires that the two files have matching characteristics. We will see what these characteristics are and how to satisfy them in later sections.

Filtering

VirtualDub bundles a number of so-called "filters". Filters are plug-ins that define a video-transformation such as resizing or blurring. Unfortunately, it is not possible to define them without any knowledge of programming languages, but do not worry yourself as we are already provided with a handful of filters by default. You can also find third-party filters, mainly on the Internet, that are compatible with VirtualDub; most of them are free but commercial ones do exist. One could partition the built-in filters into five categories using their function as criterion:

1. **Dimensions**: 2:1 reduction, crop, resize
2. **Add details/Remove noise**: static and motion blur, smoothing, 3D emboss
3. **Color**: adjust brightness/contrast, conversion to grayscale or black and white, Hue/Saturation/Value (HSV) adjust, inversion, histogram adjustment
4. **De-interlace**: field bob and swap
5. **Miscellaneous**: generic convolution, horizontal/vertical flip, perspective, rotate by an angle theta, and logo superimpose

The first category has to do with altering the dimensions of the video in a desired way. Often, we want to shrink or enlarge a video so that it suits our needs better. Also, depending on the source, the video might contains regions of black as the ones seen in DVDs and less often in TV broadcasts—those add redundancy to our video and are therefore unwanted. Rotation is not used often but it can be employed to correct a wrong recording-angle or introduce a strange-looking effect!

The second category allows you to add artificial details or remove noise that is irritating to the eye. The edges present around objects are frequently enhanced (sharpened) when the image appears "washed out". On the other hand, when noise dominates the picture, we can smoothen it out.

The third category can be used to adjust imbalances in color. An extremely dark image may be lightened by adjusting its contrast and brightness characteristics. You can also present the movie as if it was shot by an old camcorder by converting it to grayscale.

The fourth group contains functions to remove the artifacts present in interlaced video sources. Even if you are unfamiliar with this buzzword, you will have noticed the effect when playing back your captured video on a computer as most camcorders record interlaced material. The reasons for its occurrence will be explained in later chapters.

The fifth and last category is a grouping of functions that do not fit in any other group. Convolution is a method to apply a mathematical matrix to the video—the details will be explained in detail later. If you feel very creative, you can design a logo image and superimpose it over the video, as TV channels do.

If you did not find your desired effect in the list of filter groups above, I will present the exhaustive list of internal filters and discuss resources of third-party filters. Do not worry if you are not familiar with any of the above-mentioned effects—you will become familiar with them as we go through the practical examples.

Extraction of Stills

Video is all about motion but it is still composed by still pictures. Extracting stills from a video is a very common case, as it has many uses. For example, you can use a still as a preview to what the video contains when offering it for download on your website or simply to share some moments with your friends adhering to the low capacity of e-mail. Whatever the purpose, VirtualDub makes it easy to extract individual frames from a video as uncompressed or TARGA bitmaps. It is then easy to compress them in an Internet-friendly format such as JPEG. In fact, VirtualDub 1.6.0 and later, can compress directly to JPEG!

Sound Processing

VirtualDub's focus is on video but it still provides significant facilities for audio processing and they can prove to be very useful. If you have a video that was recorded in a party or a nightclub with loud music and you can barely hear the conversation, you can use a high-pass filter to cut off components of the music, making speech more audible. Cases where the sound is altogether hard to hear make perfect uses for the gain filter. Our toolbox also contains filters for:

- **Channel effects**: split stereo into middle and side signals, recombine them to stereo, combine two mono streams as stereo, split stereo into two mono streams
- **Mixing effects**: mix two or more streams into one, adjust the pitch
- **Sampling effects**: up or down sample, stretch

- **Miscellaneous**: chorus

Again, some of the above might seem a little obscure but they will be explained in greater detail later. You cannot load external audio filters in VirtualDub but the internal ones should satisfy most of your needs.

Alternatively, if you have recorded scenes where there is minimal or no dialogue between people, chances are that your video will be very dull without some music or speech narrating what is seen. Consider wildlife as an example: no matter how fascinating a video with animals is, humans still associate pictures with sound. Fortunately, VirtualDub allows you to export the audio so that you can process it externally and then re-attach (import) it. If you feel the urge to be extra creative, you can produce a completely new audio companion to your video and discard the one that came with it.

This presupposes that you have an external audio processor, however. Depending on your needs you can use Windows' Sound Recorder although that will limit your horizon to recording your voice. There are several sound-processing applications and some of them are free too—look on the Internet: you will not be disappointed.

Frame Rate Conversion

Frame rate, as the name suggests, is the rate at which frames are displayed to give us the illusion of natural motion. Quite a few years ago, when TV was first introduced, it was found that 24 is the magic minimum number of frames that had to be displayed per second for the human eye to perceive the sequence as natural motion. Three electronic standards were established: PAL, NTSC, and SECAM. PAL and NTSC are the most used ones, dominating roughly most of Western Europe and America respectively. These standards are not only used in broadcasting but also camcorders, and most importantly digital video in general.

One might ask why the frame rate of a video needs to be changed. Before I answer that, let me distinguish between the native and playback frame rate. By native frame rate, we mean the number of frames per second that were grabbed during capture, while playback frame rate is the number of frames actually played back per second on a device. For example, your camera might capture 24 fps (frames per second) content but you might have changed it to 25 fps to adhere to the PAL standard. That is not the only reason you would want to change the frame rate: the rationale may vary. You may want:

- To interchange between standards (i.e. change from PAL to NTSC)
- To "stretch" or shrink a video so that its duration matches with the sound duration and thus synchronize audio and video
- To increase the perceived quality in low frame rate videos by reducing flickering

- To perform a process called "inverse telecine" which practically converts from the NTSC defined frame rate to the native one—more on this when we talk about interlacing

Again, things are possibly not 100% clear since you have no previous experience with VirtualDub or video processing in general, but this is only the preface!

Field Interlace

This is one of the most advanced topics we are going to talk about. In many ways, it is frustrating that we still have to deal with it. Field interlace is a method that was developed for TV broadcasts in order to save bandwidth during transmission and reduce flicker during playback on interlaced devices such as TVs. Unfortunately, no matter how advantageous this might sound, it causes a visible artifact that is very annoying to the eye when viewing the video on progressive (non-interlaced) devices as shown:

You might have noticed this when playing back DVDs on your computer; it is most evident in high-motion scenes. In Chapter 8, we will study in more detail what happens with interlacing in relation to the video standards, how it is related to the frame rate, and how to deal with it.

External Processing and Frameserving

Suppose you wanted to process or play your MPEG-1 video into another application but you were unable to do so because it does not support it. You may use VirtualDub to serve frames into another application that only supports AVI files. This will not happen very often since quite a few programs support MPEG-1 nowadays, but VirtualDub frameserving can go beyond that. You can apply your video filters, import or synchronize the audio and trim the video while serving frames. This saves you the trouble and disk-space expense of saving the processed file first. You can also serve frames with VirtualDub as the client and AviSynth as the frame server. AviSynth is another free utility available on the Internet for the same purpose (see http://www.avisynth.org/). However, it has several advantages over VirtualDub:

- It can load multiple file and video formats through plug-ins
- It has an extensive library of free filters and can do all sorts of processing
- It uses a simple scripting language that makes automation easier

On the other hand, AviSynth lacks an intuitive user interface and can only deliver uncompressed video and audio. Depending on your needs, you can select the most suitable out of the two. More on this in Chapter 9.

Example Processing

There is nothing more enjoyable than learning video processing with visual aids and practical examples. Not only do you become familiar with the techniques, but you also have fun doing it. It is highly recommended that you install VirtualDub, otherwise capturing can be somewhat tedious and unpleasant since there is no potential for innovation. From here on, we enter another realm and it would be best for you to try out the examples in the text as you read through.

We are going to use a video I recorded with my digital (miniDV) camcorder in summer '04 from which we'll extract little tasks. I have imported the video on my computer through FireWire and it is stored in the DV format, taking up 4.38GB for 21:02 minutes worth of video (inc. sound). I bought the camcorder in Europe so it records in interlaced PAL at 25 frames per second. There is not much else that we need to know about the source right now. Launch VirtualDub—use the File | Open video file menu or press *Ctrl+O* to open the video you captured. You will see something like the following figure:

The left frame window displays the current frame in the video unmodified while the right one displays the same frame processed by VirtualDub. The two images are identical because we haven't ordered VirtualDub to do any processing and the source is copied over to the output. Use the slider at the lower end of VirtualDub or the arrow keys on your keyboard to seek around the video. As you would expect, this is like inspecting the video frame by frame. If you want, you can play the video by clicking on the second-from-left button at the bottom of the window, with the well-known play symbol.

As you seek through, VirtualDub displays the frame number of the image on display as well as the corresponding time in the video. In the above example, we have located frame 723, which is 28 seconds and 920 milliseconds in the video. The letter inside the square brackets indicates if the current frame is a key-frame or not; 'K' for a key frame, 'D' for a drop/dummy frame, or null otherwise.

Key frames (also known as **I-frames**) are the reference points used by some coding schemes like MPEG. Consequent non-key (also known as delta or P-frames) frames are not encoded in whole; instead, the difference between the key frame and the delta frame is stored to save space—you will learn more about this when encoding the video. DV, like other lossless schemes, has no delta frames.

The buttons at the bottom, from left to right, serve the following purposes:

1. Stop playback
2. Playback source only (same as File | Preview Input)
3. Playback source and processed output at the same time (File | Preview filtered)
4. Seek to the beginning of the video (Edit | Beginning)
5. Seek to previous frame (Edit | Previous frame)

6. Seek to next frame (Edit | Next frame)
7. Seek to the end of the video (Edit | End)
8. Seek to previous key frame (Edit | Previous key frame)
9. Seek to next key frame (Edit | Next key frame)
10. Scan backward for the previous scene change
11. Scan forward for the next scene change
12. Set current frame as the selection start (Edit | Set selection start)
13. Set current frame as the selection end (Edit | Set selection end)

You can now play with them. Use Edit | Go to or press *Ctrl+G* to seek a frame number of your choice.

Click on File | File Information. VirtualDub will display information about the audio and video parts of the file such as dimensions (width x height), length in frame and time units,the compression (if any), statistical information about the file structure (number of frames, their type and size), and finally the data rate in kilobits per second. The audio sample rate, sample precision, and number of channels are also displayed. A lot of this was already common knowledge, as we knew the source of this recording but if someone had given you a video downloaded from the Internet or otherwise, this information would have been a lot more precious.

I should make a note here that the Panasonic DV codec is available for free—a look on any popular search engine will reveal many download locations. However, you should only download it if you are interested in encoding content in the DV format, as version 1.6.0 of VirtualDub has its own internal DV decoder!

AVI Information

Video stream

Frame size, fps (µs per frame)	720x576, 25.000 fps (40000 µs)
Length	31569 frames (21:02.76)
Decompressor:	Panasonic DV CODEC
Number of key frames:	31569
Min/avg/max/total key frame size:	144000/144000/144000 (4439391K)
Min/avg/max/total delta frame size:	(no delta frames)
Data rate:	28800 kbps (0.02% overhead)

Audio stream

Sampling rate:	32000Hz
Channels:	2 (Stereo)
Sample precision:	16-bit
Compression:	PCM (Uncompressed)
Layout:	31553 chunks (0.50s preload)
Length:	40408320 samples (21:02.76)
Min/avg/max/total frame size:	2560/5121/64000 (157845K)
Data rate:	1024 kbps (0.47% overhead)

OK

A whole lot of what we have described is under the File menu—functions: append, save, save still image sequence, and the frameserver. Do not hurry to try them out; this is enough for you to know for the moment. The Edit menu provides facilities to move around the video and the selected range if any; the buttons at the bottom of VirtualDub provide a subset of those functions. Cut, copy, and paste are traditionally under the Edit menu as well.

Things get more interesting under the Video menu; that is where you can pick filters to process the video, change the frame rate, de-interlace, or select a range explicitly in frames or milliseconds. Some important settings that will be explained when the time comes are also kept there. The last group of entries allows you to copy the uncompressed bitmap of the source or even the processed output to the clipboard—much like a screenshot. The Audio menu is very similar to the Video one: only it contains settings for audio/video synchronization too.The Options and Tools menus are somewhat more advanced and they will be described in detail later. As you probably noticed, there are keyboard shortcuts for most functions in the menus of VirtualDub. There is no need to make a note of them, you will most likely memorize the ones you use the most with no special effort.

Do you feel excited? This was just an overview—we will do real business in the next chapter!

Summary

In this chapter, we introduced the processing functions built into VirtualDub. We started with the video processing functions, such as append, cut, copy, and paste. VirtualDub also contains a number of filters for applying effects to your video. We then introduced audio processing functions, external processing, and frameserving and finished with a basic example of video processing using VirtualDub and an introduction to the VirtualDub interface.

5
Basic Functionality

Let's take a closer look at the functions we mentioned earlier: namely append, cut, copy, and paste. You must be familiar with the latter as any editing package, text or image, provides them:

- **Copy,** as the name suggests will copy the selected data onto the clipboard.
- **Cut** works just like Copy, but it will delete the data from its original place.
- **Paste** will place any data that exists in the clipboard at the specified position.

They are very useful functions that allow quick editing, especially if you use the keyboard shortcuts: *Ctrl+X* for Cut, *Ctrl+C* for Copy, and *Ctrl+V* for Paste.

Open a video of your choice in VirtualDub. It is always nice to end a video edit with a scene that you really love. Most people are very fond of landscapes. Use the slider at the bottom of VirtualDub and the arrow keys of your keyboard to locate a scene of your choice. Press the *Home* key or use Edit | Set selection start to define the beginning of the range. Do not worry if you make a mistake, just repeat the steps. Then, locate the end of the scene just as before and press the *End* key or use Edit | Set selection end. If you want, you can verify that your selection is the one you actually intended by using the '*[*' and '*]*' keys to seek to the beginning and end of the range respectively. Alternatively, you may use the Video | Select range dialog, which allows you to be a bit more explicit.

Now that we have selected the scene we are interested in, we can simply copy and paste it at the end of the video. Yes, it's that simple! So press *Ctrl+C* to copy, and then the right-arrow key while holding down *Ctrl* to scroll to the end; alternatively, use the corresponding menu item under Edit. Last but not least, press *Ctrl+V* to paste the segment. You will notice a change in the length of the video from the slider. If you press Play, you should be able to see the segment we just pasted. Note that we could have pasted the segment at *any* position in the video!

Did that work? Possibly; but if it hasn't, it means that your video is compressed and you didn't copy a range that starts on a key frame, and if you cut, it didn't end on a key frame. Let me explain: click on File | Information and check whether your video is compressed or not—and if it is, with what codec. If the video is uncompressed, VirtualDub will display

Uncompressed RGB24 or something similar in the Decompressor field of the information dialog as shown in the following figure:

Video stream	
Frame size, fps (µs per frame)	720x480, 23.976 fps (41708 µs)
Length:	197 frames (0:08.21)
Decompressor:	Uncompressed RGB24
Number of key frames:	197
Min/avg/max/total key frame size:	1036800/1036800/1036800 (199463K)
Min/avg/max/total delta frame size:	(no delta frames)
Data rate:	198867 kbps (0.00% overhead)

If it is compressed, then the label will contain the name of the corresponding codec. Usually, DV codecs will have 'DV' as part of their name, in which case you will know the codec is lossless. Windows, by default, does not come with any lossless codec and if you install one, this information will be advertised—a popular example of this is HuffYUV.

If the codec is lossless, it will have no delta frames. Be alert to the odd case of a video with no delta frames but compressed in a lossy way! This is extremely rare but can happen when the video is short and has too many rapid scene changes. You can trace this if you know the compressor is lossy but the number of key frames shown equals the number of total frames. In conclusion, it is best to know the basic characteristics of the codec installed on your machine, and you can use the above heuristics to identify one if you have to.

Now that you have found out whether your codec is lossy or not you can understand the above discussion of key frames better. As mentioned previously, lossy codecs use the so-called key frames as a reference, and then encode the difference between consecutive frames to save bits. The following figure illustrates the concept:

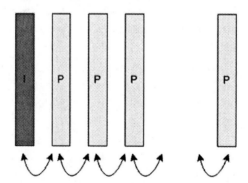

The first frame is encoded in full (Key [I] frame) while the second one encodes only the difference between the first and the second one.

Using the I-frame, the decoder can reconstruct the second frame in full. The third frame is based on the second one and so on. This can get a little more complicated if you're dealing with modern codecs like MPEG-4.

For the reasons explained above, VirtualDub cannot manipulate a range that does not start on a key frame without recompressing the whole video—the reference for consequent P-frames does not exist! Furthermore, if you cut or delete any group of P-frames that is not before a key frame, the remaining P-frames before the next key frame will not decodable. It will be explained later why this is a bad idea and should be done only when necessary. The decoder will not be able to decode the video if the key frame is not present.

I hope this was not confusing, but if it was, do not worry: there is a rule of thumb that is very easy to remember and even easier to practice. Suppose you want to use frames 200 up to 500; once you scroll to frame 200, check if VirtualDub displays [K] on the information label towards the bottom. If the brackets are empty, then the frame is not suitable; press the left-arrow key while holding *Shift* down (alternatively press the button that points to the left and has a key under it). This will make VirtualDub move to the previous key frame present in the video. Finally, press *Home* as originally instructed to mark the beginning of the selection. If you are cutting or deleting the region, also seek to the frame past your selection and confirm it is a key frame.

You can use the *Delete* key to delete the selected range from the video. Bear in mind, however, that the range will magically re-appear if it doesn't *end* on a key frame! If we delete the last P-frames of a scene (we call a scene the frames between two consecutive key frames), the I-frame is still there and the decoder can function. If we delete the I-frame and keep some of the P-frames, VirtualDub will be forced to re-insert the I-frame so that the region can be decoded. If on the other hand, you delete (or cut) P-frames that the next frames depend on, those last frames will be not be decodable; this is something VirtualDub cannot allow and therefore it re-inserts them:

Before we move on to Append, let's pause to notice something. Click on File | Information one more time and memorize the length in frames shown. Close down the dialog and notice the slider of VirtualDub; its first value is zero and its last is the length of the file. Scroll to the end of the file (*Ctrl+Right*). You will notice that the display will go blank! This is because the count starts from zero i.e. we still have 254 but the first one is 0 and the last one 253. The slider displays one extra value so that you can scroll to the end and paste or append without overwriting frame 253.

Appending

Let's do what we just did again, but this time in a different manner. As before, we want to have the range 200-500 but also save it as an independent video; let's also assume that the video is uncompressed or compressed losslessly so that we don't have to worry about cutting on a key frame. We can of course delete the [start, 199] and [501, end] ranges but that would be superfluous, since VirtualDub provides this for us. Select the range; if you don't remember how, flip back a couple of pages. Select Video | Direct Stream Copy and finally click on File | Save as AVI or press *F7*. Define a filename and click Save.

Now we possess a video with just the scene we are interested in so we will append it to the end of the original video to achieve the same effect as before. Click on File | Append AVI Segment and select the file you just saved. VirtualDub will add it to the end of the video or pop up a verbose error message similar to the following image if the videos are incompatible:

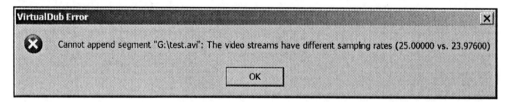

Now you know how to use the basic functions for video manipulation! If you want to manipulate a range that does not start on a key frame, these functions will fail for the reasons explained above. However if you absolutely must do it, you could re-encode to another format and extract the range you are interested in, save it, and finally append it to the video. You will learn how to handle the encoding in a later chapter and also find out why this is not a great idea.

One might wonder why VirtualDub can't cut, copy, or paste between different videos/windows. That is a very reasonable question. Well, for one, video data would be very large indeed to fit on the clipboard and although that could be dealt with, operating on one file guarantees that the conditions enabling two videos to be merged are met:

- The two videos have the same dimensions (width and height)
- The frame rate is the same
- They are compressed with the same compressor
- In strict video formats like MPEG-4, both videos are compressed with the same standard features and parameters

The reasons are straightforward; imagine trying to fit an A4 sized piece of paper in a letter-sized envelope. You would have to fold it first. In the same way, you would have to convert one of the videos to match the characteristics of the other. You will be able to do this after reading the following chapters.

Extracting Stills

Saving still images of your video can be very useful if you want to automate processes like making thumbnails of a video file to post on the Internet. Using VirtualDub, you can extract the stills and use a batch file to automate the thumbnail creation.

You can extract the stills of the whole video if you like, but beware of the file sizes; VirtualDub can export to Bitmaps (uncompressed) and TARGA/JPEG (compressed). In either case, the collection might occupy a lot of disk space depending on the frame size, length, and compression quality. Try to limit the operation to the specific range in which you are interested. You can select the range you want using your chosen method.

When you have selected the region of interest, select File | Save image sequence. The following configuration dialog will appear:

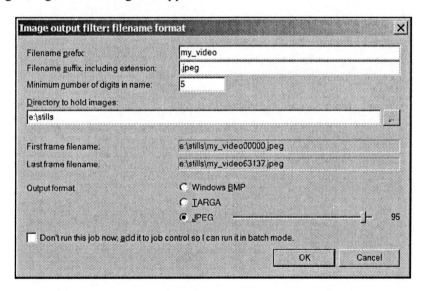

Start by selecting the output format—BMP, TARGA, or JPEG. If you are using JPEG, adjust the quality factor (over 90 will give high-quality stills). Secondly, use the browse button to locate the directory to hold the images.

Adjust the minimum number of digits to satisfy the number of frames in the selected region of the video; e.g. for 240 frames use three, or for 63137, use five. Type in a prefix to indicate the source of the stills—depending on the directory structure you may be able to leave this blank. You can preview the filename that will be formed with your settings in the two labels First frame filename and Last frame filename. Finally, when you are happy with your settings, click OK for VirtualDub to begin saving the stills. Note that:

- This operation will save the stills of the processed output and so, if you want to save stills from the original, make sure you have not applied any filters.

- The numbers are relevant to the region and not the whole video! Thus, the first still will always be number 0.

- The previews of the filenames will not take into account the range you have selected; they will always reflect the whole video.

Summary

You have been introduced to some of the most basic functions of VirtualDub and have acquired the knowledge required to:

- Cut, copy, and paste
- Append and delete
- Work with codecs that use key frames
- Extract still images

The next chapter will introduce the core VirtualDub filters.

6

Video Filtering in VirtualDub

Chapter 4 listed a number of video filters that VirtualDub provides; the time is right to familiarize ourselves with each one of them using practical examples. So far, we have only learned how to add, insert, or delete fragments of the video; we will now learn how to manipulate the actual video content using filters. Filters are entities that, given an input, will produce a well-defined output that is going to be different from the input in some well-defined way. For example, a water tap filter will receive water from the main water distribution pipe as input and after cleaning unwanted substances from the water (function of the filter) will give an output of drinking water! Going back to the world of video processing, after you have read this chapter, you will know how to:

- Set up a sequence of filters to achieve the desired effects
- Configure each filter independently and tweak it to best serve your purposes:
  - Clean up rough or grainy videos
  - Add details to blurry sources
  - Make the motion of the video smoother when moving objects appear to be "outside of the picture"
  - Create a cool 3-D looking emboss of your video
  - Flip or rotate
  - Produce negatives of the video
  - Cover a portion of a video with a color
  - Superimpose your home-made logo
  - Convert to black & white or grayscale to "age" your video
  - Fix the colors of a video that does not look natural
  - Change the dimensions or remove the black bars from the sides of the video
  - Add subtitles
- Add more filters to your collection

Filters compose a large piece of the functionality that VirtualDub provides, even more so since you can add third party filters and there are numerous free filters available on the Internet! Details will be provided later.

How Filters Work

Filters could be seen as small plug-in programs that integrate mathematical or logical procedures. Some of them work on a per-frame basis while others have different temporal dependencies. Resizing and histogram adjustment are examples of the first category while de-interlacing and motion blur (which depend on more than one frame in time) belong to the second category. They are very useful because:

1. They can be combined in a chain fashion (the relative order can be important) applying various effects without producing more than one output.

2. They are easy to use although they provide essential functions.

3. They are modular so you can easily add or remove them.

4. Many of them are free. Check out `http://neuron2.net/`.

Pipelines

It is always useful to understand the notion of the pipeline. It sounds too technical to be easily understood, but in fact, it is a very simple concept to grasp. Let us suppose that we want to distribute our video over the Internet, but since our web-space provider allows only a few megabytes of storage, we have to shrink the video as much as we can.

We also want to increase the brightness of the video because it looks dark. In this case, we crop, resize, and finally adjust the brightness in that order (three filters). It is natural that the input video is first cropped, and then fed into the resizing filter and the brightness-adjusting filter; the final output video is the output of the brightness filter.

The figure below demonstrates the generic case of a pipeline like the one we just made, this time with an arbitrary number of filters:

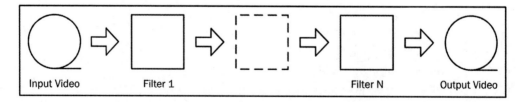

| Input Video | Filter 1 | | Filter N | Output Video |

The process illustrated above takes place in the memory; the pipeline defines how the frames are circulated after they have been read and before they are encoded and saved. The above diagram does not take into consideration the processes of retrieving and saving the frames. The following figure demonstrates the series of events more clearly:

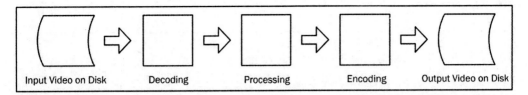

| Input Video on Disk | Decoding | Processing | Encoding | Output Video on Disk |

The input video is read from disk and decoded if it is compressed and the specified processing, including filtering, is applied. The output of the processing is then encoded and saved back to the disk.

One might ask why it is necessary to decode the video before it is processed; it would be much simpler to process the encoded video and not have to re-encode it later.

The answer is pretty simple: compressed video cannot be altered. To achieve compression, the video is transformed into a representation unsuitable for processing. So the only functions possible are to delete and add as we saw in the previous chapter—and even those can be achieved only under strict rules. This is also the reason why it is very important not to re-encode the video in-between filters and to minimize the processing in general (more on this in Chapter 8).

Why is the Order Important

Another common question is: why is the particular order of filters being placed in a pipeline important? The truth is that it is not always important; it depends on the filters applied. Remember your mathematics teacher: he or she must have, at some point, taught you that (3x5) +9 is not equal to 3x (5+9). In the same way, the order in which the filters are applied can determine the result. That does not mean the difference is always visible, but there are often good reasons to do it in a particular way. For example, it is best to crop and then resize since the resizing filter will have less work to do as the image will be smaller and the black regions will not interfere with the rest of the processing. On the other hand, if you want to flip the image and then blur it, the order is insignificant: the same output will be produced either way.

Built-In Filters

VirtualDub (1.6 or later) includes 32 built-in filters for your convenience; they can be divided into categories as shown in the following table:

Category	Filters
Dimensions	2:1 reduction
	Cropping (often via Null transform)
	Resize

Category	Filters
	Rotate by 90, 180, or 270 degrees
	Rotate by an arbitrary angle
Add details / Remove noise	Blur (radius 1 or 2 Gaussian)
	Box blur
	Chroma smoother
	Emboss
	Motion blur
	Sharpen
	Smoother
	Temporal smoother
Color	Brightness/Contrast
	Grayscale
	Hue/Saturation/Value adjust
	Invert
	Levels correction (also known as histogram adjustment)
	Threshold
De-interlace	De-interlace
	Field bob
	Field swap
Miscellaneous	Fill with color
	Horizontal / Vertical flip
	Convolution
	Logo superimpose
	Perspective wrap
	NTSC TV data conversion

Have a look yourself:

1. Open a video of your choice.
2. Click on Video | Filters (alternatively press *Ctrl+F*).
3. Press Add.
4. From the list that pops up, select a filter and click OK.
5. Repeat until you are satisfied with the filters in the pipeline.

You could load external filters during step 5 by clicking on Load. As I explained earlier, the order is important most of the time and mistakes can be made. In that case, you can use the Delete button to remove a filter completely or the Move Up and Move Down buttons to re-arrange its relative position in the list. Intuitively, the filter at the top of the list is the first in the chain to process the input:

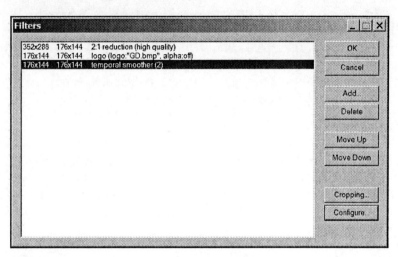

The screenshot above displays a sample filter chain; notice that:

- There is no cropping filter, but the Cropping button becomes available once you add your first filter.

- The input and output video resolutions of each filter are displayed. For example, the first filter receives the original video size (352x288) and halves both width and height (2:1 reduction) giving output dimensions of 176x144. If you have not loaded a video, VirtualDub will assume 320x240 dimensions.

- When you add a filter, an additional dialog pops up on occasion with configuration content. This allows specifying parameters of the filter, if any. If you make a mistake in the configuration of the filter, you can revisit the settings by selecting the filter and clicking on Configure. The parameters chosen are displayed next to the name of the filter.

As you see, there is nothing complex to this and some things that might seem obscure are there for good reasons. The cropping functionality is arranged like this because of its trivial nature. Having a separate filter for cropping would add unnecessary complexity to the processing; VirtualDub handles it very smartly. When you want to crop, you simply alter the portion of the video that a filter will accept as input! If you have no other processing to do, you may add the Null transform filter, which as the name suggests, has no effect on the video: it simply copies the data from input to output in order to modify the video dimensions by cropping. This technique avoids copying the data when not necessary and allows a significant speed increase.

Next, we'll take a closer look at the filters and explain how to use them to achieve a desired effect.

Smoothing and Blurring

A very crowded group of filters is concerned with smoothing out noise in the picture or blurring it, either to produce a hazy effect or to remove unwanted details. VirtualDub provides the so-called Gaussian blur, box blur, and motion blur as well as a smoothing filter with two variations: temporal and chroma smoother.

Gaussian Blur

The "blur" and "blur more" filters of VirtualDub are examples of Gaussian blur, with radius 1 and 2 respectively. In general, the radius determines how strong the effect is. Greater radius results in more blurred image while lesser radius results in less blurred image. The following figure demonstrates the effect:

Original Image   **Gaussian Blur**   **Gaussian Blur (Radius 2)**
                            (Radius 1)

It does remove details of the image, but this can be useful, especially with camcorder recordings; sometimes the image appears undesirably grainy for various reasons. In the following example, the reflection of the sun on the seawater creates a grainy and blocky effect, which I removed using the soft (radius-1) blur filter:

Original Image   **Blur Filter**

Box blur is a customizable version of the Gaussian blur; it blurs blocks (boxes) of pixels. The following configuration dialog will pop up upon adding it:

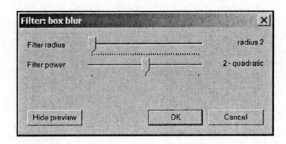

From this dialog, you can manually control the strength of the blur. The Filter radius increases the radius of the blur while power determines the number of passes: 1-box, 2-quadratic, and 3-cubic. Click on Show preview after you have opened a video file:

- Move the radius slider at values 10, 20, 30, 40 and 48.
- Each time you change the radius, move the power slider, and observe the effect of box (1), quadratic, (2) and cubic (3).

It should be quite clear now that this filter can do some extreme blurring which is not going to be of use very often.

Smoothing

You have probably noticed that the effect of blurring, if taken to the extreme, resembles pictures that look out of focus. The preferred way to remove noise without washing out the picture or removing too many details is smoothing. Not only that, but the smoother filter gives you more control over the level of effect. If you add the Smoother filter to the list, you will see the following dialog:

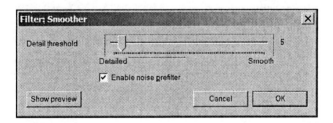

Click on the Enable noise prefilter setting—this will apply Gaussian blur to the smoothing operation. The Detail threshold setting allows you to specify the strength of the smoothing; most people tend to like the result that a threshold in the range of 0-10 gives, but the slider goes up to 100. You should try it to see what works best for your eyes; some people appreciate a sharp and crispy image while others prefer a smooth one.

Smoothing tends to preserve the edges because of its thresholding nature. For instance, in the example I presented when talking about Gaussian blur, smoothing (threshold of 5) would have very little effect:

Before Smoothing   **After Smoothing (Threshold-5)**

What you see above is the input and corresponding output from smoothing with a threshold of 5. Even though the skin areas and the chair now appear smooth and less pixelated, the edges are very well preserved and the image does not appear "washed out".

The temporal smoother has a similar strength setting. As the name suggests, it takes into consideration multiple frames in time in order to smooth the image. It is therefore smarter than the normal smoother, which works on a single-frame basis, and it can be useful to get rid of noise present on some, but not all, of the frames. Such artifacts are produced by TV reception for example; in general, when recording video, you will get some persistent noise. Be careful, however, as extreme temporal smoothing can result in blurred motion or "ghosting"! Always preview your videos before saving them.

Chroma smoother is a special filter for codecs that reduce the number of samples in the chroma components of the video to achieve better compression. The components are up-sampled when the video is decoded, usually by repeating the values of nearby pixels. The technique is used by most if not all MPEG codecs and this filter uses a more intelligent algorithm to do the up sampling. You will not need this unless you are working with a compressed source or if your capture card outputs native YUV (more on color spaces later). The "TV" filter of VirtualDub is a different flavor of chroma smoother and works with the YIQ color space native to NTSC.

Motion Blur

Motion blur is the effect that is evident in photographs where the target object was moving while the film was exposed to light (what we commonly call a "shaken" picture) or when the exposure was long.

It is also evident in video when things are moving too fast; often it's not visible when the video is playing, but it is certainly evident when paused. For example, look at the frame opposite: the landscape is blurred while moving the camcorder swiftly. That is of course the natural effect and this filter is designed to simulate it:

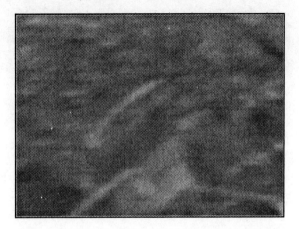

There are no configuration options for this filter so you would only need to add it to the list of filters. In case you are wondering what good this filter might be, you can use it when moving objects in the video appear to be "out of the picture". This side effect is especially noticeable in computer animations that have not been motion blurred. Film studios use motion blur when they shoot a scene in a studio set with a fixed color background (green is popular) and then artificially add a landscape to mix the two in a natural-looking way.

Sharpen

The exact opposite of smoothing is sharpening: it attempts to add details in a blurry image by enhancing the edges of the pictures. Similarly, the configuration dialog of the filter has only one slider to control the strength of the effect as you can see below:

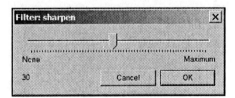

The output is straightforward and is demonstrated in the following pictures—a weight of 30 was used (an extreme value in most cases):

Original Image   **Sharpened Image**

Note that this filter incorporates no intelligence; if you try to sharpen a compressed video that has many blocking artifacts, the blocking will be enhanced as it cannot distinguish between artifacts, noise, and edges. Therefore, avoid using this filter in video with noise or other artifacts.

Emboss

Emboss will convert the edges and gradations in the picture to shades, producing a 3D-like emboss effect. It can have a very entertaining and playful end product—give your creativity a go! The configuration is quite simple as shown below: the left group of buttons control where the light source is while you can control the strength on the right. An additional option for a more rounded output is also present:

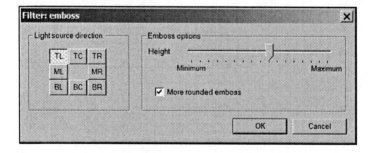

The light source requires familiarity with 3D graphics, so try to visualize a spotlight in the scene before the conversion is done. It controls how the surfaces will be embossed; consider the examples opposite:

the image on the left was created with a Top Left (TL) light source direction while the image on the right was created with a Bottom Right (BR) light source direction. As you can see, the direction of the embossing is reversed.

Original Image

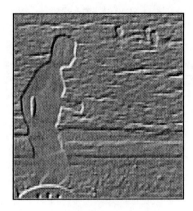

TL Light Source

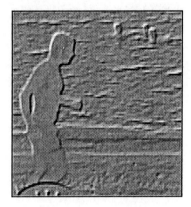

BR Light Source

Flip

VirtualDub offers two filters for horizontal and vertical flipping; they will simply swap the left and right or top and bottom respectively.

Since a picture is worth a thousand words, the following images display the effect:

Original Image   **Horizontal Flipping**   **Vertical Flipping**

Rotate

VirtualDub offers two filters for rotation, one for fixed angels (90°, -90°, and 180°), and another that will work for arbitrary angles. Two versions exist since the standard rotations are very easy to perform quickly with specialized algorithms while an arbitrary angle rotation requires a generic algorithm. The respective configuration dialogs are as follows:

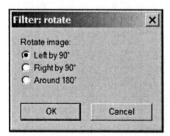 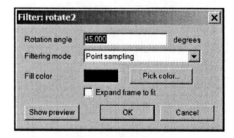

The rotate filter is very simple to use: you simply select the rotation angle out of the three options, and you're set. Note that rotation by 180° is not equivalent to vertical flip! Can you see why? Check it!

In a similar manner, for the rotate2 filter you need to define the rotation angle up to three decimal points. The filtering mode defines the interpolation method used to apply the rotation to the image: point sampling, bilinear (2x2), or bicubic (4x4). With rotation, the output still needs to be rectangular, so there are areas that do not contain any portion of the video. The Fill Color refers to those areas. By default, the rotated picture is centered and some areas are naturally excluded; you can force VirtualDub to expand the output frame so that it fits the whole of it by selecting the Expand frame to fit option. The following pictures demonstrate the difference between the two, using a 30° angle:

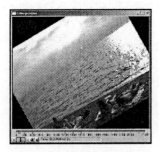

Image Rotated by 30° **Expand Frame to Fit Enabled**

Invert

Pixel values range from 0 to 255 for the RGB (Red-Green-Blue) color space. Inversion is as simple as subtracting each pixel value from 255 and storing it back. This results in an inversion of colors as evident in film negatives: white becomes black etc. as shown in the following example frame:

Original Image **Inverted Image**

You can also use the filter to reverse the effect if you already have an inverted video.

Color Fill

This is a very simple filter indeed: it just replaces a portion of the image that you define with a specified color. It might be useful to cover objects such the registration of a car or even a person that you do not wish to be seen. This requires that the object is not moving, so fast-moving videos are not an option; however, with a bit of imagination you can use it for other purposes too.

Here's how to control the fill filter: once you add it to the list of filters, the following dialog pops up:

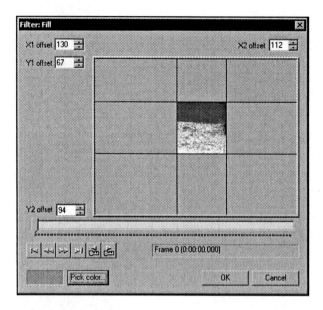

You will notice a slider and related buttons at the bottom as usual, and four spin controls: two at the top left, one at the top right and a last one at the bottom left of the dialog. Those controls define and set the rulers that set the portion of the image to be filled.

An **offset** is a number that specifies how far in the image a ruler is (in pixels), counting from the corresponding edge. The X1 offset is the distance between the left border of the image and the left ruler, in pixels. The Y1 offset is the distance between the top border and the top ruler and so on and so forth.

Two things are initially awkward for most people in this dialog:

1. The portion of the picture shown is actually the part that is going to get filled with the color specified and not the part of the video that will be visible.

2. The up and down buttons of the spin controls move in the direction of the image not in the direction of the corresponding number. For instance, pressing down for the Y1 offset, will not decrease the offset number as expected, but will move the ruler *down* and therefore increase the offset.

Do try to use this filter to make sure how the configuration is organized. For the above example, the output image would look like the following picture:

Often, you can use this filter to remove watermarks or logos from a video if they are too far in the image and you cannot remove them by cropping the image.

Superimposing a Logo Image

Especially when publishing edited footage on the Internet, it is very useful to super impose a logo on the video indicating who the author is or how this video was created and edited. VirtualDub 1.6 and later can read Windows Bitmap (.bmp), TARGA (.tga), and JPEG files (.jpg, .jpeg—as of VirtualDub 1.6.0). I used an image editor (Windows' Paint will do) to create a 300x100 pixels logo as shown in the following figure:

Edited with Virtualdub!

Adding the filter to the chain results in the following configuration dialog. Browse the image you want to superimpose; if it contains alpha information, it can be used for per-pixel blending. In the latter case, enable the option—it will then be possible to use the other two options available: pre-multiplied alpha and secondary image for alpha. The first is to be used when the alpha channel of the image was created at the same time as the rest of the image. You can also define a secondary image whose gray channel will be used as alpha information.

filter: logo

Logo image	G:\virtualdub_book\ch10_31.bmp

☐ Enable per-pixel alpha blending using alpha channel
☑ Use premultiplied alpha
    Premultiplied alpha is best when the alpha channel is created with the
    image; blend the color channel against black when creating the logo.
    Non-premultiplied alpha is better if the alpha channel is created separately.

Alpha image   ☐ Use gray channel of secondary image for alpha channel

Opacity   45%

Justification					
TL	TC	TR	X offset	0
ML	MC	MR	Y offset	0
BL	BC	BR		

Hide preview   OK   Cancel

The controls in the bottom half of the dialog allow you to control the transparency
(Opacity) and position (Justification) of the image. 100% is opaque and 0% is transparent.
The buttons that control justification use 'T', 'M', 'B', 'L', 'C' and 'R' for top, middle,
bottom, left, center, and right. 'BC' places the logo at the Bottom Center:

Convolution

Convolution is a method very often used in image processing and it involves the
modification of each pixel's value in relation to the value of its neighbor pixels. This
involves the use of a matrix, called the **kernel**; it can be of any size, but the most
common is 3x3 as this involves only the adjacent pixels.

Some very simple mathematics is required in order to understand how it works—a simple example would suffice. Suppose we have the following image portion to process using the 3x3 kernel shown on the right. The pixel of interest is at the center:

46	50	59
64	58	52
60	58	50

0	-1	0
-1	5	-1
0	-1	0

Convolution will update the value of the pixel by calculating the value:

$$x = \frac{46 \times 0 + 50 \times (-1) + 59 \times 0 + 64 \times (-1) + 58 \times 5 + 52 \times (-1) + 60 \times 0 + 58 \times (-1) + 50 \times 0}{0 + (-1) + 0 + (-1) + 5 + (-1) + 0 + (-1) + 0}$$

The region defined by the pixel in question and its neighbors is multiplied by the 3x3 kernel (dot product). Then, the elements of the results are summed and divided by the sum of elements of the kernel. If we call the 3x3 matrices p (pixels) and k (kernel), then the target pixel x is equal to:

$$x = \frac{\sum_{i=1}^{3} \sum_{j=1}^{3} p_{i,j} \times k_{i,j}}{\sum_{k=1}^{3} \sum_{l=1}^{3} k_{k,l}}$$

As you can see the process is fixed and generic; the kernel is the most important factor as it defines how the new pixels are calculated. The kernel used in the example above can be employed for sharpening, although you should prefer the dedicated sharpening filter. A search on the Internet using the keyword "convolution" will reveal many other kernels that you can use. Another common example is the following kernel, which achieves blur:

1	1	1
1	1	1
1	1	1

The general convolution filter in VirtualDub works a little differently.

Assuming matrices p and k as above, the target pixel x is equal to:

$$x = \frac{\displaystyle\sum_{i=1}^{3}\sum_{j=1}^{3} p_{i,j} \times k_{i,j}}{256}$$

Mathematically, this means the value is not normalized using the kernel sum, but a fixed value, 256. Intuitively, it means you can control the output brightness/intensity level through the coefficients of the kernel. To maintain the same brightness level, the sum of the kernel coefficients must be equal to 256 as shown by the mathematical expression:

$$\sum_{i=1}^{3}\sum_{j=1}^{3} k_{i,j} = 256$$

If this condition is not met, then the following ratio determines the level change:

$$\frac{\displaystyle\sum_{i=1}^{3}\sum_{j=1}^{3} k_{i,j}}{256}$$

If it is greater than one, the intensity is increased; if less than 1 then it is decreased. Note that we divide by 256 and not 255 because the range [0, 255] has 256 members. To get back to practical examples, the above blur kernel is *approximately* translated to

28	28	28
28	28	28
28	28	28

in VirtualDub. The reason this is only an approximation is that 256 is not divisible by 9: it has a remainder of 4. As a result, the brightness gain is approximately 0.984 and therefore the level is going to decrease by a small amount. You could overcome this problem by replacing four of the coefficients with 29; although this would give a perfect gain of 1, it would give greater weight to those pixels. The compromise is not visible, but it is good to know when you are designing your own convolution filters.

The configuration dialog is intuitive; it allows you to edit the kernel and define a bias. The bias is a value that will be added to the pixel value after applying the kernel. You can enable clipping, which is a process that validates that the output is in the range [0, 255]. If it is not, the pixel values will overflow resulting in an erroneous result.

You have to worry about this if the absolute value of your gain is greater than 1. In any case, it is always good to enable it, preview the video, and finally to disable it, making sure the output is the expected one. Disabling clipping makes the filter faster. If you test the output as described, do make sure you preview parts of the video that are very dark and very bright, as overflow is likely to happen when the pixel values are close to the boundaries of [0, 255]:

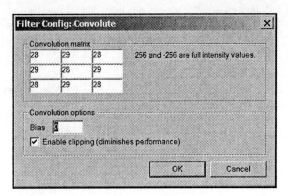

Grayscale and Black & White Video

If you want to make your video look old, then this filter is for you. It converts color to tones of gray giving an old-fashioned look to the video. Many people consider still photos in grayscale to be more artistic—a theory that could be extended to video.

More extreme effects can be achieved using the threshold filter, which only allows two tones of gray: black and white. The name of the filter is threshold because it uses a threshold to assign black or white to each pixel. If a pixel's value is higher than the threshold it becomes black or otherwise white.

Remember that lower values are darker (R=0, G=0, B=0 is black) and higher values are brighter (R=255, G=255, B=255 is white). The configuration dialog is very simple:

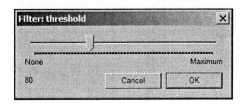

The following figures demonstrate the grayscale and black-and-white effects:

Grayscale Effect

Black and White Effect

Brightness/Contrast and Hue/Saturation/Value Adjustment

Lighting is often not ideal when video recording an event and this fact can affect the brightness and/or contrast of the footage. This filter is designed to alter the brightness and contrast in order to fix those problems. Adjusting the brightness will affect how dark the video looks while adjusting the contrast will alter the difference between the brightest and darkest parts of the picture.

There is nothing magical about this filter and its configuration (shown below): try different combinations of brightness and contrast and observe the effect. Using this filter yourself is the best way to determine the best values. There is no magic formula, just go with what looks best to your eyes!

High Brightness

High Contrast

The **Hue/Saturation/Value** model was developed to make it easier to adjust the respective components in an image. **Saturation** is the strength of the colors, or more formally, refers to how saturated they are. An image with low-saturation colors looks like grayscale while an image with overly saturated colors will look unnatural. Check that by adding the HSV adjusting filter and dragging the Saturation slider to the right.

In order to understand the notions Hue and Value/Intensity, it is necessary to visualize the following HSV model:

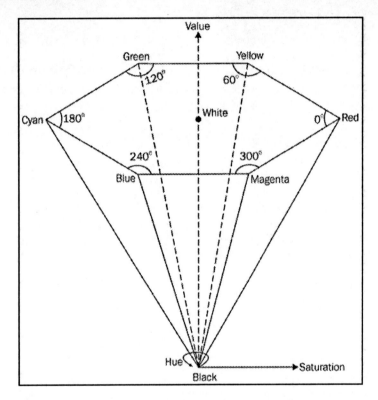

It is a shape similar to a cone, but its top is in fact a hexagon. Each corner of the hexagon is closest to red, yellow, green, cyan, blue, and magenta starting from 0 degrees and in 60 degrees increments. At the bottom there is black and at the top (the center of the hexagon), there is white. 'S' stands for Saturation; as expected, saturation is equal to zero in the vertical axis. Increasing the **Hue** will make the image more yellow, or green, etc. **Intensity** (also called **Value**) ranges on the vertical axis and controls the brightness.

High Saturation   **Low Saturation**

The levels filter provides even more control over contrast and brightness as well as gamma correction. The configuration dialog is shown below:

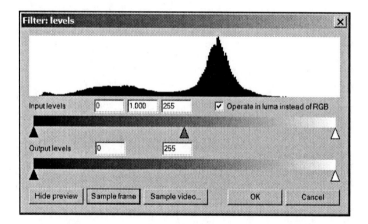

It is a wise choice to have the Operate in luma instead of RGB enabled (default); this means that the chroma information of the picture will not be affected i.e. hue and saturation are preserved. This process is also used in image processing and goes by the name histogram equalization. Do not worry if you have never heard of this before, or have no idea what it is: I am about to explain.

The top slider has three parameters designated by arrows; the first and third represent the black and white levels respectively. Values lower than the black level become black while values higher than the white level become white. The middle parameter applies gamma correction: intuitively, it controls what becomes middle gray (half-way between black and white) in the image. Notice that black and white do not change when applying gamma correction.

The bottom slider is labeled output levels because this process is done in steps: first, the black and white levels are adjusted (input settings), then gamma correction is applied, and finally the image levels are scaled down to the levels indicated by the bottom slider to give the output. In other words, the parameters' function is the same as in the top slider, but applied at a later stage.

Cropping and Resizing

Before we continue with the specifics of cropping and resizing, it is essential to understand the notion of **aspect ratio**. As you might imagine, it is the ratio of width over height. In mathematical notation:

$$aspect\ ratio = \frac{width}{height}$$

A lot of the time, this is given. For example, video recorded by my camcorder has an aspect ratio of 4:3 (4 units across to 3 unit's height), although the size is 720x576. Calculating the aspect ratio from the pixel resolution would give 5:4, which is not correct. This is because the pixels are not square in most analogue devices; the pixel aspect ratio is not 1:1 and it is not the case on computer screens. Because of this, you will need to know the aspect ratio beforehand or, guess it!

Often it is necessary to resize i.e. change the dimensions of a video, usually to increase the coding efficiency and therefore reduce the size of the output. Other reasons include conformance to video standards; if you plan to burn your video onto PAL VideoCD for example, you will need to have a resolution of 352x288. Another way of reducing redundancy is to crop the black bars of a video. Either way, the codec will have less information to encode.

In the process of cropping and resizing it is essential that the aspect ratio is maintained so that objects do not appear squashed or stretched in any way: more on this shortly.

Black Bars Wrapping the Video

There are many subtleties that common display devices like TVs and monitors hide in order for us to have a pleasant experience. Even then, it might not be satisfactory for some people: let me explain. Consider the following frame:

It was captured from a music video broadcast and as you can see there are thick black bars above and below the picture itself. Widescreen DVDs have added black bars at the top and bottom as well. Those bars are removed by widescreen TVs in a process called cropping; other types of TV systems display them.

Now let us take the picture without the black bars and resize it to the dimensions of the whole frame as it would be displayed on TV. The result is as shown:

It is possibly not visible at first, but if you try to compare it against the original image, you will see that it is vertically stretched. This is a logical consequence since we had to fill the space previously occupied by the black bars.

This example demonstrates that:

- When the image is a lot wider than its height—what is advertised as 16:9 in DVDs—but is played on a TV with different dimensions (4:3 aspect ratio), it is necessary to pad it with black bars to fill the extra space. Note that in some cases, 16:9 content is converted to 4:3 by cutting the additional parts of the image and as a result, a large portion of the video is not visible.

- Removing the necessarily added black bars by cropping will alter the image dimensions and therefore the aspect ratio. Attempting to resize the picture to the original dimensions so that it will fill the whole screen would result in unnatural-looking pictures as shown above.

- The aspect ratio is a characteristic of the picture that should be kept constant throughout changes in the dimensions. This way the objects are preserved as intended; an example that demonstrates this concept is the image of a circle. If you resize the image to a smaller size without respecting the aspect ratio, the circle turns to an ellipse as shown:

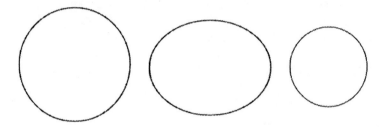

The original circle is the one on the left; the resized circle is in the middle with no respect to the aspect ratio and the properly resized circle is on the right.

Cropping Black Bars from the Video

Doing the actual cropping is trivial. All you need to do is visually define the regions to be cropped out. You can crop the input of any and every filter in the chain if you like, although it's not required. Note that cropping does *not* alter the aspect ratio of the video.

Press *Ctrl+F* for the filters dialog to pop up; you will see the Cropping button at the bottom right. It is disabled if there are no filters in the chain or none of them is selected. If you are wondering what happens if you do not wish to apply any filtering to your video but wish to crop, that is what the "null transform filter" is for. Let us see how it's done.

Add the null transform filter and select it: finally press the cropping button. The following dialog will appear:

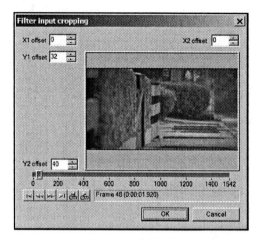

We have seen the same layout when we examined the color fill filter. Four rulers (left, right, top, and bottom) control the portions of the image to be cropped out. Before you get on with specifying the offsets, scroll to a position of the video that has bright colors near the borders. This will help you distinguish between black that is actually part of the image and the black bars. Usually it is sufficient to crop on top and bottom, but there are thinner black bars at the left and right sometimes. The new dimensions of the video (after cropping) will be displayed in the input size of the filter you applied the cropping to.

The most important thing here is to define even numbers as offsets assuming that the original size is made of even numbers (width and height). That said, you should always ensure that the output dimensions are even.

Without delving into too much detail about this, it is a safety measure that you should use: some codecs and filters *assume* that the dimensions are divisible by 2 and do not deal with predicaments with odd number dimensions. In fact, if you are not going to resize the video (see below), you should make sure both the width and height are divisible by 16. The rationale for this is that most recent codecs (MPEG-4 etc.) work on a 16x16 macro-block basis and might produce erroneous results if the input video is not sized accordingly.

Resizing

The process of altering the size of a video without altering the content of the picture (i.e. without cropping) is commonly referred to as **resizing**. This can mean that we are either expanding or reducing the size of a given video.

Common reasons for resizing are:

- Burn to Video or SuperVideo CD (VCD, SVCD respectively) or another standard that defines the dimensions of the video.
- Reduce the number of bits required to encode the video at a given quality.
- Increase the quality of the video with the specific bit rate/number of bits available.

Before going into the specifics of VirtualDub, we need to know how to calculate the new dimensions with respect to the aspect ratio of the video and the "divide by 16" rule. Prepare yourself to see a couple of mathematical equations in the following text; I promise, however, to provide shortcuts to make it easier.

Suppose the width and height of our video are w and h respectively. The next step is to find out the aspect ratio and crop any black bars:

- TV broadcasts are commonly 4:3, but the contained picture might be 16:9 with added black bars. In this case, we crop the bars to retrieve the original 16:9 content.
- If the source is a true 4:3 TV broadcast, there might be an allowance of about 8 pixels that we can crop from each side.
- DVDs usually list the aspect ratio among other technical characteristics at the back of their case.
- In any other case (arbitrary source), you need to guess what the aspect ratio is, given the above facts.

To define the new resolution you will need to decide on a new height (h_n, but make sure its division with 16 is perfect (there should be no remainder), e.g., 640. Then, the new width (w_n) will be:

$$w_n = aspect\ ratio \times h_n$$

Verify that the new width is a multiple of 16. If it is not, you will need to play with the cropping parameters or select a new height h_n until you get it right. Now that we have the dimensions to which we want to resize, let us see how that is done.

Press *Ctrl+F* to load the filters chain dialog. Add an instance of the resize filter: the configuration dialog is:

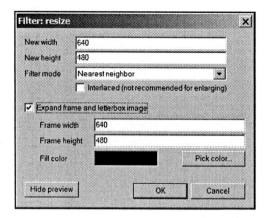

The options are self-explanatory: you input the new width and height you calculated previously in the corresponding fields. You also have the chance to add black borders to the image by enabling the Expand frame and letterbox image option and entering the desired frame dimensions.

Because of the size change during resizing, the pixels of the source and output image do not necessarily match. Therefore, it is required that a mechanism exists to fill in the missing pixels if we are enlarging the picture or to combine the pixels if we are shrinking it. VirtualDub offers eight different variations of such algorithms:

- **Nearest neighbor**: This is the simplest and fastest method of all since it simply chooses the nearest source pixel. Too often, the fastest method is not of the best quality. This resizing algorithm has "sparkling and chunkiness problems", according to the author of VirtualDub.

- **Bilinear and Precise Bilinear**: This is somewhat smarter than the nearest neighbor, but most people think that its output is blurry. The precise version of the filter should be used when shrinking to avoid artifacts.

- **Bicubic and Precise Bicubic**: This has a sharper output than bilinear, but will produce ringing artifacts when enlarging. When shrinking the image, the precise version should be used. There are three different modes for this algorithm: A= -0.6, A= -0.75, and A= -1.0. As the constant 'A' decreases, the sharpness of the output increases. You should be aware, however, that the sharper the video is, the harder it is to encode for most codecs—maintaining a balance is a compromise.

- **Lanczos3**: This produces slightly better results than Precise Bicubic, but is a bit slower and produces stronger ringing. It is the preferred method of many amateurs whose goal is to have high quality video rather than fast processing.

What works for me or for someone else might not work for you. Appreciation of crispness and quality is entirely subjective and you should give all the methods a go to see what pleases your eyes the most.

Also, it is generally accepted that enlarging a video is not a good idea; the data is expanded and by definition, errors will be produced as the expansion is only based on estimation. Having said that, it is even better if you do not have to resize at all; resizing is, however, necessary in many cases so do not feel it's forbidden. Do make sure that there is good reason, if you are enlarging.

The 2:1 Reduction filter will halve both the width and height of the video, but the two filters are deprecated and should not be used.

Subtitles

Subtitles allow you to display text while your video is being played back. This can be to:

- Translate foreign dialogs to the native language of the viewers
- Make ambiguous dialogs or whispering clear
- Add comments

There is really no limit to what you can do with subtitles nor should you restrict yourself; the great thing about home-made videos is creativity!

Many methods exist to insert subtitles to a video; you can specifically:

1. "Burn" the subtitles in the video or in other words, make them part of the video at the pixel level
2. Attach them to the video as a text stream.
3. Attach them to the video, externally, as text; this means they are not contained in the same file, but can be displayed using additional software

Naturally, each method has its own advantages and disadvantages; the main ones are presented in the following table:

Method	Advantages	Disadvantages
Burn-in	No additional software required for playback—subtitles will be displayed on every machine that can play the video Single file output	Only one language can be embedded Lack of editing capability for both the subtitles and the video itself Degradation of video quality Font family and size and position of subtitle display cannot be changed

Method	Advantages	Disadvantages
Attach in container	Single file output Can embed more than one language No effect on video quality Allows the subtitles to be edited Allows font and position to be changed during playback	Editing can be tedious (requires de-multiplexing the subtitles to edit and then re-multiplexing) Additional software (subtitles) required for playback—anyone without it will be unable to view the subtitles
Attach externally	Subtitles are standalone & totally optional Can embed more than one language No effect on video quality Allows the subtitles to be edited easily Allows font and position to be changed during playback	Additional software (subtitles) required for playback—anyone without it will be unable to view the subtitles

Burning the subtitles in the video does not restrict you from editing it. The video is still composed of frames and frames are still composed of pixels; however, burning the subtitles will mask some of the video and more importantly, performing for example a blur or smooth operation will affect the subtitles as well, possibly smearing the video. As you can see from the table above, burning the subtitles in the video has more disadvantages than advantages!

Embedding the subtitles as text and reproducing them requires, as stated above, some third-party software. Fortunately, all packages are free just like VirtualDub; what you need is:

- Sub Station Alpha from http://www.eswat.demon.co.uk/ to create or edit the subtitles
- AVIMux GUI from http://www-user.tu-chemnitz.de/~noe/Video-Zeug/AVIMux%20GUI/index-eng.html to multiplex (abbr. mux)
- VSFilter from http://sourceforge.net/projects/guliverkli/ to display subtitles
- The VirtualDub Subtitler filter from http://www.virtualdub.org/virtualdub_filters/ if you decide to "burn" the subtitles in your video (not recommended)

Sub Station Alpha (SSA) comes with an installation wizard, which is very straightforward to install; just double-click on the executable and follow the instructions. AVIMux GUI, like VirtualDub, is just a bunch of files in a ZIP archive that you can extract anywhere you like. If you are going to use the VirtualDub Subtitler, load it from the filter dialog for the moment; you will learn how to permanently install filters shortly.

VSFilter on the other hand requires some special attention: once you extract the ZIP archive, you get two directories named `Release` and `Release Unicode` respectively. If you are on Windows NT/2000/XP/2003 use the Unicode version; if not, use the plain one. Each directory contains a DLL library; you need to copy it to a directory from which it will not be deleted (`c:\windows\system32` is a good one) and type `regsvr32 VSFilter.dll` from that same directory, using the command prompt. Alternatively you can use the *Run* facility from the *Start* Menu; you will need to be more explicit for that to work—`regsvr32 c:\windows\system32\vsfilter.dll`. A message box should pop up confirming that registration was successful.

Creating the Subtitles

Writing subtitles by hand can be very tedious and difficult at times. Some subtitle creation utilities allow you to play the video at the same time and manipulate it accurately to ease the process. Sub Station Alpha (SSA) employs an even easier method; it will read an audio file (WAV) and allow you to select parts of it, reproduce them, and define the subtitle text for it. It may sound like an impossible task to do at first, but with minimal training you will be able to add subtitles very quickly. Some users have reported that they can perform faster than real-time!

So we first need to save the audio from the file in a format that SSA can read and process. Launch VirtualDub and open the video. Then, follow these steps:

1. Select Audio | Full processing mode.
2. Select Audio | Compression and ensure that the <No Compression (PCM)> entry is selected. Press OK.
3. Select Audio | Conversion or press *Ctrl+O*. Select 8-bit Mono output as shown opposite and click OK.
4. Select File | Save WAV and define a filename for the audio to be saved.
5. If you want to process the video further, select Audio | Direct Stream Copy or if you do not wish to edit the video, change the conversion settings to No change. In other words, revert to the default audio settings so that they do not affect the rest of the processing:

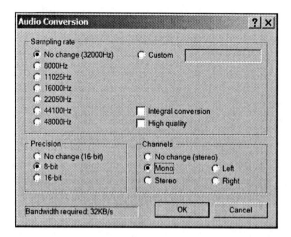

Normally, uncompressed data is very large, no matter whether it is video or audio. However, 8-bit Mono will take up 1-2 megabytes of space for each minute of video. Note that for this process to work, you will need to do this as the final step; if you add or remove any portions to/from the video, then the subtitles' timings will be wrong! So do this only when you have finished with editing.

Now that we have the audio, we can open it in SSA and start adding the text. Launch SSA and select Timing | Time from WAV file; a new group, as shown will replace the top controls:

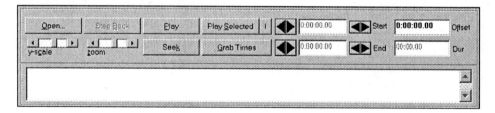

Press the Open button and select the WAV file we just extracted out of the video file—a waveform of the file will be sketched. Use the y-scale and zoom settings to scale the waveform vertically or zoom into it respectively. Click on some point with the left mouse button and press Play to playback the part of the file starting at that point.

Now, left-click at the beginning of the file (yellow mark) and press Play. When one phrase is spoken, press stop and right-click at that point to define the end of the range (red mark). Click Play Selected to verify the selected region and, if you are satisfied, type the text you want to appear at the text field below. If not, adjust the yellow and red marks to your liking by using the arrows on the left side of each time field.

Finally, press Grab Times and the first so-called event will appear at the list below as shown. To insert a new line, use \n:

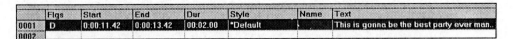

	Flgs	Start	End	Dur	Style	Name	Text
0001	D	0:00:11.42	0:00:13.42	00:02.00	*Default		This is gonna be the best party ever man..
0002							

Repeat the above steps until you have scanned the whole video and your subtitles are complete. At that time, click on File | Save As and save the subtitles you just created. A dialog will pop up, allowing you to define optional information such as author and title.

The default appearance of the text is controlled by the *Default style and is somewhat unusual (yellow and small letters). Use the Styles | Define option to adjust it according to your preference.

There are many more things you can do with SSA, such as sliding or rolling text, but those features are outside the scope of this book; for more information, consult the SSA help files.

Burning the Subtitles in your Video

This is the part where you just feed the subtitles to VirtualDub and it burns them to your video. Follow these easy steps:

1. Launch VirtualDub and open your video if you haven't done so already.
2. Open the filter chain dialog and load the Subtitler filter.
3. Add the Subtitler filter to the chain and when the configuration dialog pops up, point to the .ssa file we created earlier.
4. Alter the settings to your liking and press OK:

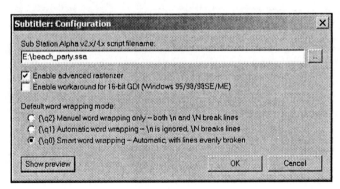

The subtitles will now appear in the right-hand side window (output) as shown:

If you realize you have made a mistake in the subtitles, correct the text in SSA and load the configuration dialog of the subtitler filter in VirtualDub, so that the text is reloaded.

Multiplexing Subtitles in AVI using AVIMux GUI

It is just as easy to multiplex your subtitles into the AVI file itself. It also gives you the freedom to add the subtitles *after* you have encoded the video!

Launch AVIMux GUI. The list at the top will contain all the files you want to join into one AVI i.e. the video file and the subtitles. You can drag and drop the files onto the list, or alternatively you can right-click and select Add. Either way, add the AVI file and SSA files. Then, select the AVI file and press the generate data source from files. The state of AVIMux will now be similar to the following screenshot:

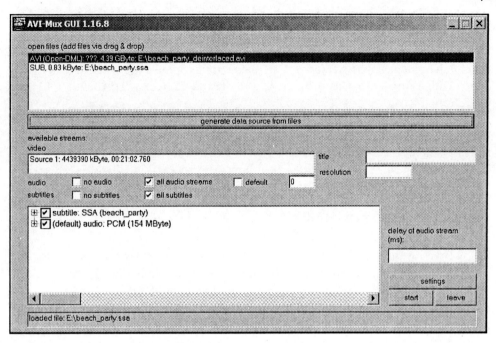

Everything is set; press start to select the output file and begin the multiplexing process.
Every time you play back the video, assuming you have installed VSFilter, an icon will
appear on your taskbar as shown. If you right click on the icon, you can access settings
related to the display of the subtitles:

If you wanted to edit the subtitles, possessing the final output, you could drag the icon in
AVIMux, then right-click on the subtitles' stream and use the corresponding menu
function to save them. Consequently, you could edit and re-mix them into the video.

External Subtitles

Alternatively, you can have your subtitles externally. This requires that the subtitles and
video file have exactly the same base filename! For example, my_video.avi and
my_video.ssa. Once you play back the video, VSFilter will take control of the SSA file.

Adding More Filters to Your Collection

You can find many free filters on the Internet to add to your VirtualDub filter library. The VirtualDub homepage has a filter section that contains some extra filters that are not shipped with VirtualDub. Check `http://www.virtualdub.org/virtualdub_filters/`.

Another shrine for VirtualDub and AviSynth filters is Donald Graft's homepage at `http://neuron2.net/`.

The installation process goes from easy to non-existent for filters. Once you download the filter, usually contained in a ZIP file, follow this process:

- Unzip the archive and locate the file with `.vdf` suffix.
- There is usually an HTML or plain text (`.txt`) file with information and instructions on how to use the filter.
- If you want to use the filter on rare occasions or just want to try it out, launch VirtualDub and press *Ctrl+F* to bring up the filter chain dialog. Use the Load feature to locate and load the filter (point to the `.vdf` file).
- If you are satisfied with the results and want to have the filter available every time you launch VirtualDub, locate the directory where you have placed VirtualDub. You should see a subdirectory named `plugins`; if not, create it. Finally, copy the `.vdf` file from the archive to the directory. The filter will be available in the list of filters you can add the next time you launch VirtualDub.

Now you have a complete view of the filtering system within VirtualDub. You have seen the possibilities of what you can do and know how to extend them by adding third-party filters. Most filters serve very specific purposes, but a lot of them have more generic purposes and can therefore be combined to produce very artistic effects!

Summary

I hope you have enjoyed playing around with the filters of VirtualDub; they will make your life easier and far more interesting by adding to the pool of the possibilities when it comes to video editing. In this chapter we have seen:

- How to distinguish between temporal and non-temporal filters
- How to combine them into pipelines to create effects or correct imbalances
- How to pick the filter for the correct purpose and configure it properly

Furthermore, we learned where to get more (free) filters and how to add them to our collection. Next, we are going to learn some of the more advanced features of VirtualDub that allow us to manipulate the frame-rate, remove interlacing artifacts and so on.

7
Professional Video Editing

There is a bunch of filters in the Video | Filters menu. So why do we need extra plug-ins for VirtualDub, especially where some of them are similar to internal VirtualDub filters?

In some situations, applying an internal filter for optimizing an image will not lead to good results (because of the internal algorithm, video format, etc.). In such cases, we can try other filters that do the same job in a different manner. Moreover, not all tasks can be performed with VirtualDub internal filters and we have to use other plug-ins instead.

The plug-ins discussed in this chapter:

- Remove unwanted logos, dates, and areas from video: **DeLogo, Logo Away, and Region Remove**
- Provide quality handling like noise removal (**Chroma noise reduction, Dot Crawl**) and ghost removal (**Exorcist**)
- Do fun and artistic actions on video like simple transitions (**FadeFX**), half toning (**Halftone**), rotating between various colors (**Hue Cycle**), converting video mode from color to color bands (**Luminescence**), and making videos look like old movies (**MSU Old Cinema**)

These filters have their own characteristics and developers. For each, a link to download directly from the developer's website has been provided. I have used the latest versions, but I strongly recommend that you check the provided links for newer versions.

Installing a New Plug-in

Installing third-party plug-ins is fast and easy. Just copy any **VirtualDub Filter** (VDF) file to the PLUGIN directory at the location where you've installed VirtualDub.

To view a list of existing filters (including default and third-party plug-ins), go to Video | Filters and press the Add button in the Filters dialog box.

Another approach is to address your plug-in directly inside VirtualDub (so that copying the VDF files to your application is not necessary). Just click on the Load button in the Add Filter box and locate your plug-in.

As you can see, the word [internal] appears in front of the default filters. For third-party plug-ins, the plug-in developer's name is displayed:

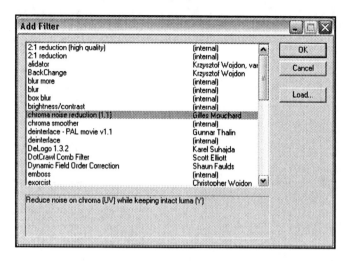

Logo Removal Filters

While capturing video from analog resources, especially TV channels, there are often logos or other information such as date, time, and name on the images. Sometimes we prefer to erase all this from our video. Many plug-ins have been developed to achieve this goal. Let us try some of them.

Logo Removal with DeLogo

The **DeLogo** plug-in (delogo132.zip) developed by Karel Suhajda can be downloaded from http://neuron2.net/delogo132/. This filter features two logo removal techniques. Logos have either semi-transparent or solid colors. For removing semi-transparent parts of an image, we have to use the **DeBlend** feature of the DeLogo plug-in.

This feature works with a given alpha and color mask. DeLogo has an analyzer that uses this data to compute the color of pixels behind the logo and redraw them at that position. When dealing with solid logos on an image, the DeBlend technique fails.

In this situation, we have to use the **Repair** property. The solution used in this technique is very simple. Based on colors of pixels around the opaque part, some computation is made and the color of target pixels set.

Removing Solid Elements from an Image

Let's use the DeLogo plug-in to remove the date and time from the following video:

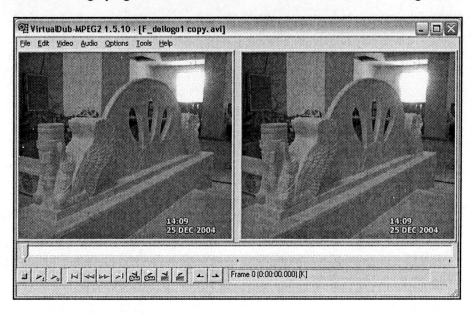

Take a screenshot from the current frame by pressing the *Alt + Print Screen* keys. (You can use any application to capture image from video.) Copy the captured image in an image-processing program, such as Photoshop. We don't need any professional editing so we can even use MS Paint. Now, paint on the time stamp with red color (ff0000).

For better results, paint some extra pixels around the time stamp. The quality of this plug-in's output depends on two factors: the pixels that you specify and the background.

These extra pixels help the Repair algorithm figure out the color of pixels at target area. We have to paint enough extra pixels to provide the algorithm with the required data. We also have to paint extra pixels near enough to the logo to prevent the algorithm from getting confused with too much information:

After painting the pixels, save the file as a 24-bit .bmp image and name it F_dellogo mask1.bmp.

Notice the number at the end of the file name. You can choose any other name for your mask file, but you have to put a number at the end of the file name so that VirtualDub can recognize the file and make it a part of the video stream.

Now choose Video | Filters and press the Add button. Select DeLogo from the next dialog box. In the Mask properties group of the following configuration window, click on the Load button next to the Repair radio button and load the mask file:

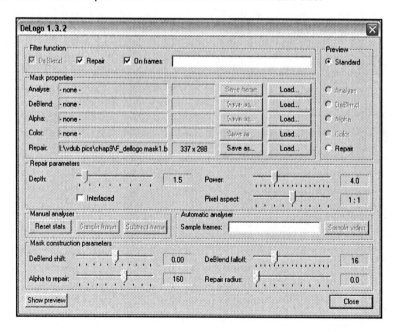

To see the result immediately, click on the Show preview button and you will find that the time stamp has disappeared from the image:

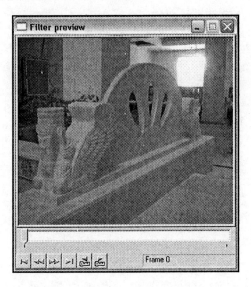

For further fine-tuning, use the other controls in the Repair parameters group. To see the result of changing these sliders select the Repair radio button in the Preview group:

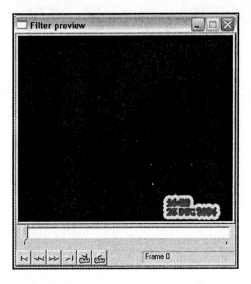

When you get the desired result, click on Close and then OK to return to the VirtualDub preview area. Save the result by selecting File | Save Image Sequence.

There are other functions in the Mask properties group for various situations; these will be used later. For example, for removing alpha blended elements we can combine various parameters together to get a good result.

Removing Alpha-Blended Parts of a Frame

Alpha-blended elements are semi-transparent parts of a frame that may contain information about a video.

Look at the following frame. There is a semi-transparent horizontal bar at the top with some additional solid information (like logo and time stamp) on it. We are going to clear any unwanted bars and logos from this frame and obtain the original image pixels:

Press *Ctrl+F* and select the DeLogo filter. In the Configure box press Show preview. Now in the Mask properties group, click the Save frame button next to Analyse and set a name for the captured .bmp image.

Open this image in MS Paint and draw a red (FF0000) box around the top logo bar. It's recommended to make this red rectangle a few pixels greater than the original bar. DeLogo will use this rectangle as a masked area.

Leave a small horizontal bar at the bottom of the logo bar empty and draw a blue (0000FF) rectangle covering the rest of the frame. Save the file.

The empty (original) rectangle will be used as a reference area. In fact, DeLogo will use the color information of these pixels for reconstruction of other pixels.

Any pixels of the frame located in the blue rectangle will remain unchanged. The DeLogo plug-in treats blue color as "safe and permanent", and so does not analyze this region at all:

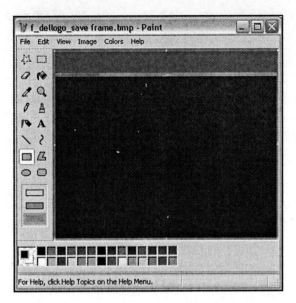

Go back to the DeLogo configuration box and click on the Load button next to the Analyse section of the Mask properties group. Now load the mask .bmp file that you have created.

Notice that both Analyse and DeBlend sections are initialized now. When we select Analyse from the Preview group, the red and blue rectangles remain unchanged, but the original area turns to black. By contrast, when we select DeBlend from the Preview group, the red edge fades a little in the original area as shown in the following screenshot.

With the **deblend falloff** slider we can change the amount of fade area. This slider specifies the pixels that can be used in the plug-in for finding out the color of other pixels in the removed area:

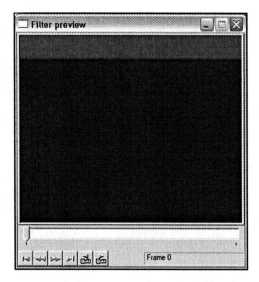

Now it's time to analyze the top logo bar. Click on Sample Video and select All frames from the next dialog box. In this way, we'll be sure that analyzing will be done with the maximum accuracy (although for long videos this process may take a long time).

Selecting the first option provides fastest analyzing, but decreases accuracy. The second option works on video key frames only. So this provides a balance between the two previous options:

If the top bar does not appear on the whole video, you must manually specify all frames to be processed in the Automatic analyser group in the Sample frames input box:

If your logos still exist on the current frame, change the sliders in the Mask construction parameters, especially Alpha to Repair. Close the window.

We have some solid logos on the horizontal bar at the top of the frame. For removing them we must use the previous technique. Capture the frame. Mark the solid parts with red. Save the file. Press *Ctrl+F* and then double-click on the DeLogo filter to open the configuration box.

Click on the Load button next to the Repair section, and load the mask bitmap file. Clicking on the Show preview button will show the following image (you may do any necessary fine-tuning with the sliders):

The removed area does seem blurry, but that is the price we must pay for clearing the video of unwanted logos!

An Easier Way of Removing Logos

DeLogo is a powerful filter that can help us in clearing images professionally. However, for achieving a good result we have to spend a lot of time tuning DeLogo controls and editing external images.

Sometimes we want to erase simple logos from a video fast and easily. The **Logo Away** plug-in is one of the fastest and easiest-to-use filters for doing this. This plug-in was developed by Kryzstof Wojdon and offers six ways of removing unwanted logos. You can get this plug-in from http://republika.pl/vander74/virtualdub/index.html.

The removal mechanism in Logo Away works by analyzing the neighboring pixels of a selected region and reconstructing the selected area based on this analysis.

The Fastest Way of Removing a Logo with Logo Away

Here is the situation: we want to clear the comments from the following image:

Press *Ctrl+F* and then the Add button and select Logo Away from the list. There are many controls and options in this box. Click on the Show Preview button so that you can monitor what happens while changing the settings.

Now look at the middle part of the controls. Two groups contain options for setting the size and position of the area to be removed. Point on one of these options' up arrow and hold down the mouse button. Notice the change in the removal area. The removal area in this plug-in is a blurry rectangle, which is computed based on the surrounding pixels.

In this way, you can figure out the function of each control in these two groups. Set a rectangular area around the logo. It is recommended that the removal area be a little bigger than the logo itself. For our example, the settings are:

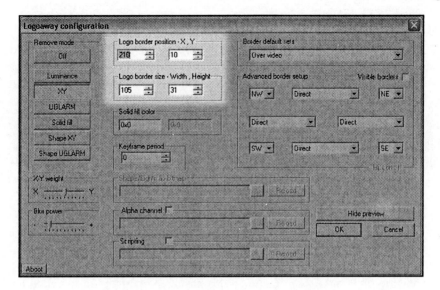

The result is:

There are two sliders at the bottom left of this box. They set the direction (X or Y-axis) and amount of blurring. Use them for different images to get the best results.

Using Other Logo Away Controls

There are other controls in the left section of the Logo Away configuration box, which help us to remove logos by various methods. For example, if you click on the Solid fill button, a solid rectangle with the color that is set in Solid fill color box will be placed on the specified region.

You can set the rectangular area for removing unwanted parts. Click on the shape XY button on the left and select the bitmap image and related alpha channel in Shape/Lightmap bitmap and alpha channel boxes respectively. This filter will affect the pixels specified in the shape image and its alpha channel.

More Convenience in Removing Logos

We are now familiar with the various techniques used for removing unwanted parts of an image using external plug-ins like DeLogo and Logo Away. Both plug-ins, based on complex algorithms needed for removing logos, have a complicated professional interface and are CPU intensive. Shaun Faulds has developed a plug-in called **Region Remove** for removing unwanted elements from videos in a simple manner. The Region Remove filter can be downloaded from:

http://www.videohelp.com/download/regionremove-v1.zip.

This filter has a simple interface. Look at the following image. We are going to remove the text from this video using the Region Remove filter:

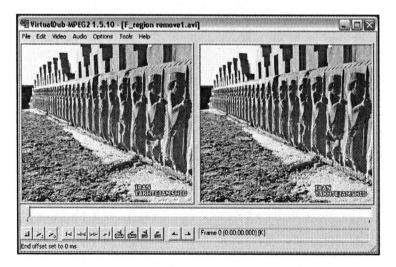

Press *Ctrl+F* and then Add and select the Region Remove Filter:

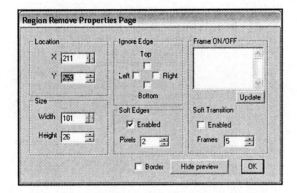

Click on the Preview button to monitor the output while making your settings. Now, with the controls in the Location and Size groups, set the position and dimension of the area to be removed.

In the Soft Edges group, we can soften the edges of the removal area so that the pixels in this area fade from the original background to the colors computed by this plug-in. This gives a better result. Choosing greater values for Pixels in this group will increase the softness limit. For removing the logo properly we need to increase the size and change the position of the region to be removed. Based on the image and logo we are dealing with, we have to select a proper combination of options in the Location, Size, and Soft Edges groups to get a good result. This filter has a special ability that was absent in the previous two plug-ins. In the Frame ON /OFF group, we can:

1. Set the frames that have unwanted regions on them
2. Set a transition between frames that have unwanted regions and clear frames in the video

The settings done in the previous image make the edited frame look like the following screenshot:

Putting Desired Information on the Video

We have learned how to remove unwanted elements from our video, but how do we put our logos or other information on frames? With the **Logo** filter, we can insert any image on video frames and set the location and alpha channel for them. It is an internal VirtualDub filter and you can read more about it in Chapter 6.

Let's try something different. Assume that we want to put a live timestamp (time and date) on a video while capturing or exporting in VirtualDub. The Logo filter can insert still images on frames, but what we need is a filter that works with the system clock and inserts the current time and date into the video. A useful plug-in that does this has been developed by Christopher Wojdon, and is called **Alidator**. You can download it (`alidator.zip`) from:

`http://www.republika.pl/vander74/virtualdub/index.html`.

The time stamp will be inserted at the bottom of the frames horizontally, like this:

Image Processing Filters

It's not unusual to have unwanted noise and shadows in captured videos. Several plug-ins have been developed for improving video quality.

Decreasing Color Noise with CNR

One of the effective and useful systems of representing color data is the YUV color space. In this color space, Y is the luminance (brightness intensity) and U (chrominance 1) and V (chrominance 2) are the chroma components (the difference between a color and a chosen reference color of the same luminous intensity). The YUV system is used mainly with video (TV program transmission, VHS recorder, MPEG) whereas computers use the R'G'B' system.

One of the usual artifacts in video capturing is color noise, and with the **CNR** (Color Noise Reduction) filter, we can reduce the noise on chrominance. This can be done without affecting the luminance factor so that the video quality is preserved.

The CNR filter (cnr11.zip) developed by Gilles Mouchard can be downloaded from http://freevcr.ifrance.com/freevcr.

The Algorithm Behind This Plug-in

CNR uses a simple formula to detect and reduce color noises on frames. It uses the variation (X axis) and coefficient (Y axis) of the current frame and the previous frame to figure out the blend required for representing colors.

In the Tips group, selecting low values for each channel's diagram helps us to find scene changes more precisely. By contrast, higher values will remove color noises from each frame, but the accuracy of detecting frame changes will decrease.

The controls in this filter are simple and easy to use. There are two horizontal (x) and vertical (y) sliders for each channel. Tune these sliders until you get a suitable result for your video:

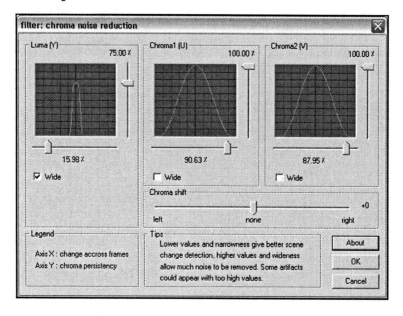

If there are some shadows on the video, colors spread on the left, and a purple tape appears on the right edge of the frame use the Chroma shift slider. This control moves color signals to the horizontal position that you want.

There is another filter doing the same job and developed specially for NTSC videos. **Dot Crawl** is a plug-in for removing crawling dots and false colors caused by NTSC composite videos. This plug-in developed by Scott Eliot can be downloaded from the following link:

http://home.earthlink.net/~tacosalad/video/dotcrawl.html.

Removing Shadows from Video

Sometimes while capturing a video (especially from TV channels) some shadows appear on the video. Various factors cause this artifact (such as bad channel settings, stormy weather, or an airplane flying above your TV antenna). We recommend the **Exorcist** plug-in (exorcist.zip) developed by Christopher Wojdon, available at http://www.republika.pl/vander74/virtualDub/index.html/, for removing these ghost signals.

On selecting this filter for a shadowed video, we will see the following options. Press the Show preview button to see what happens while changing the controls:

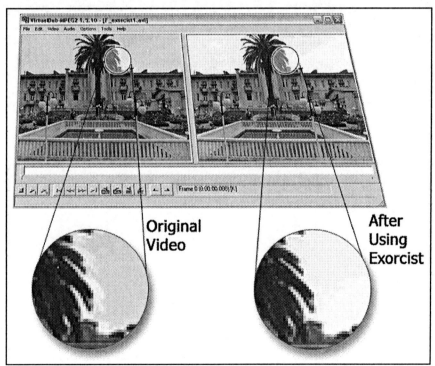

In the Ghost shift group, we can change the position of shadows horizontally. Move this slider until you get the correct position for the ghost. If the intensity of shadow does not match the original video, change the Ghost intensity slider to make it darker or lighter than before.

Here is a sample usage of this filter. As you can see, the shadows on the original video seen around large objects (around the tree branches, for example) were eliminated after using the Exorcist filter:

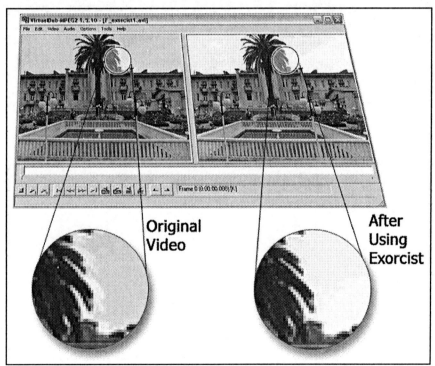

Professional Video Editing

Filters for Fun

The filters discussed until now improve image quality and eliminate unwanted parts from a video. But some filters simply insert special effects on the video. Even in VirtualDub we can find examples of such filters, but here we will discuss external plug-ins.

Defining Simple Transitions for Video with FadeFX

FadeFX is a plug-in for adding transition effects like fade in/out to videos. This filter (fadefx.vdf) can be downloaded from http://home.earthlink.net/~tacosalad/video/.

This plug-in has simple settings. Just specify the frames you wish to add the effect to in the Effect range group and then select the transition type from the Fade parameters group. Checking the Extend effect box will expand the effect to subsequent frames:

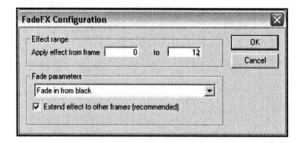

There are five options for fading in the FadeFX plug-in. You can see the effects in the following image:

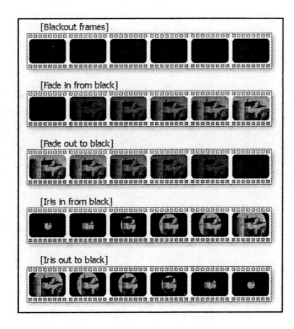

Half Toning Video

Half toning means representing an image in circles with two solid colors and Tom Ford has developed a plug-in named **Halftone** that does this job for us. You can download this filter (halftone.zip) from the link http://compsoc.net/~flend/virtualdub/halftone.html.

Here is the effect of this filter:

In the HalfTone settings box you can set the Spot and Background colors and specify the precision of the block and the intensity for half toning. The Show Preview button can be used to display the results while changing these settings:

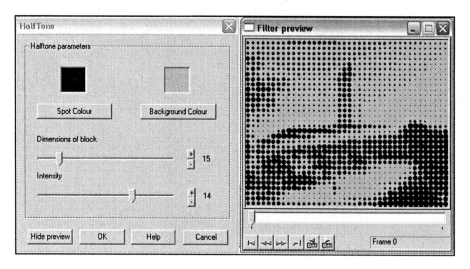

Fading between Various Hues

Another amazing plug-in developed by Tom Ford is the **Hue Cycle** filter (huecycle.zip). With this we can cycle between different hues while playing a video. Hue Cycle can be downloaded from http://compsoc.net/~flend/virtualdub/huecycle.html.

There are two sliders in the Hue Cycle window. The first slider set the frames needed for a full cycling. The other slider specifies whether a displacement from the video colors is needed at the beginning of cycling:

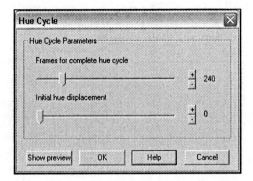

Colorizing it More

Need more colors on a video? The **Luminescence Band** plug-in might help you. With this plug-in you can define the number of lightness bands (luminescence), change hue position, set the color saturation, and finally reduce the number of colors in the video:

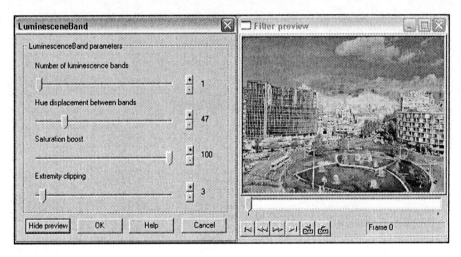

You can find this plug-in (`lumband.zip`) at the following address:

`http://compsoc.net/~flend/virtualdub/lumband.html`.

Pixellate Effect

This is another effect that is used to make a video look like a color checkerboard. Just set the size of the pixel blocks and it figures out the number, color, and size of the required squares for an image:

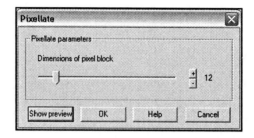

This **Pixellate** plug-in (`pixelate.zip`) can be downloaded from:

`http://compsoc.net/~flend/virtualdub/pixellate.html`.

Here is an example:

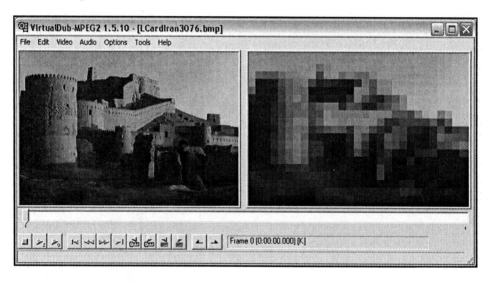

A 1920's Cinema Plug-in

Would you like to edit your videos so that they look like an old movie? OK, then use the **MSU Old Cinema** plug-in.

This plug-in (`msu_oldcinema.zip`) developed by the MSU Graphics team can be downloaded from `http://compression.ru/video/old_cinema/src/`.

There are some presets in the MSU settings box, which simplify the process. You can try them in the Preset drop-down list. However, if you wish to configure the controls manually, here is a brief description:

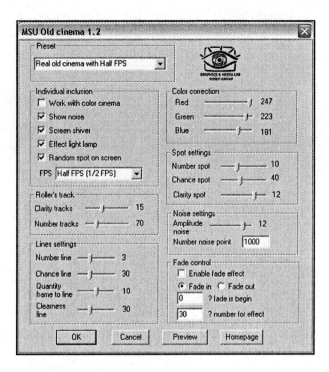

In the Preset group, you can select a preformatted setting for your video. All basic tasks are done in Individual inclusion. These tasks include defining B/W or color cinema, showing or hiding noise, light lamp, spots on screen, and shaking the image. Moreover, you can specify all these settings for whole video frames or for parts of them in the FPS drop-down list.

In the Color correction group, use the sliders for the video hue settings.

In old videos, there are usually some short vertical dark lines that look like rain drops. We call them tracks and for simulating them, we use the Roller's track group.

Almost all old videos have complete vertical lines that can be drawn in the Lines settings group. For showing spots and noises, use the related groups on the right.

We can specify the range of frames in which this filter will be active in the Fade control group. We can define a fading effect for this plug-in at the start or end of its action. Here is a sample usage of this filter:

Summary

In this chapter you were introduced to a few external VirtualDub plug-ins. There are many more plug-ins and filters on the Internet and the number is ever increasing. For those interested in programming, source code for the filters is available (in C++) at the provided links.

Now you know:

- Installing these plug-ins is quick and easy.
- They can be categorized in different groups based on their functionality.
- Some of them are used for enhancing and optimizing video quality.
- Some of them are used for removing or inserting visual elements on videos.
- Some of them are used for applying some artistic effects to videos.

Always bear in mind that there are always alternative methods for doing a particular process in VirtualDub. Besides, there are situations that VirtualDub can't handle internally. So try the solutions given by third-party plug-ins sometimes. Just copy them into the VirtualDub plug-ins folder and they will be at your service.

8

Advanced Topics

Now that we know the basics of applying filters to our video and more, it is time to delve into some of the more advanced topics such as frame rates and interlaced sources. We will look into the details of converting from one format to another (also known as transcoding) and understand how it fits in with processing/filtering.

After reading this chapter, the following will be clear:

- Why analog television is the way it is and how digital pictures have inherited from it
- How to append videos of different formats by changing the frame rate of the source video
- How to change the playback rate
- How to change the number of frames per second of video to reduce the processing complexity or for other reasons
- How to control the editing process efficiently to preserve video quality and save processing time

Color Television

Previously in this book you have seen the word NTSC, which might have looked like another obscure and cryptographic acronym for something that was designed to make your life harder. This section aims to explain what NTSC and PAL are, why they exist, and what they imply when processing video from NTSC or PAL sources. (DVDs ship with NTSC or PAL video only.) What I have not mentioned before is a third standard named **SECAM** that is used in a few countries around the world.

NTSC stands for National Television System Committee; the committee introduced a TV standard sometime in the early 1950s that inherited its name. The standard was aimed towards color television and, naturally, it aimed to satisfy compatibility with black and white devices and signals. In simple terms, a color TV should be able to decode a monochrome picture signal and vice versa, a black and white TV should be able to decode a color transmission without any modifications. This requirement resulted in the YUV color space: a separation of brightness (what a black and white device would display) and chroma. NTSC, PAL, and SECAM are not fundamentally different from one another—they are variants of the same concept.

SECAM advanced on NTSC and exploited the response of the human eye to chroma information for the first time. Humans are less susceptible to detail in the chroma domain while they perceive changes to brightness as more important. Therefore, SECAM transmitted one line of pixels for every two in the original picture—at half resolution. The standard was revised a few times, thus rivaling NTSC, which evidenced problems with hue: colors displayed would be slightly different each time.

Only France adopted SECAM, where the standard originated; the rest of Western Europe adopted PAL—a new standard that corrected the problems with NTSC. Each standard has its own advantages and disadvantages, but in a nutshell:

- PAL and SECAM display 25 frames each second while NTSC displays about 30 fps (29.970 exactly). This means that NTSC is superior to the other two when it comes to motion flicker—it is less visible.

- NTSC displays only 525 lines versus the 625 of PAL and SECAM. Thus, the resolution of NTSC is inferior.

Frame Rates

Practically, NTSC is associated with unpleasant eye effects. This is not because of the reduced resolution, but because the original film material is shot at 24 frames per second and then converted to the corresponding standard—PAL/NTSC/SECAM:

- Film video is usually transferred to PAL/SECAM (25 fps) by speeding up the video by approximately 4.2%. The effect of the speed is virtually invisible to most of us. Some, however, find it disturbing.

- On the other hand, it is more difficult to convert NTSC. The individual lines that compose each frame are divided into two interlaced sets (the odd and even lines), which we call fields. A process called 3:2 pulldown then creates extra frames by repeating one field from a frame with the complementary field from the following frame. So some frames will contain fields from two successive frames in the film video, between which motion may have occurred. Again, this can be disturbing for a number of people.

Converting between the standards can be very tedious, but also necessary. The complexity of the task lies in the many possible variations. Video content should preferably be watched in the format that it was encoded for; but if a conversion is required, VirtualDub provides the means—3:2 pulldown removal and frame-rate change. However, let's start with the basics.

Changing the Playback Speed of Video

It was stated earlier that the 4% (approximate) increase in playback speed introduced in PAL is not obvious to most humans. Let's run a fun experiment that will teach us how to perform this change. Find your favorite 1-minute long PAL video or video segment, change its frame rate to 24 fps, and see if you notice the difference.

Launch VirtualDub and open the video. Then:

- Check Video | Direct Stream Copy so that no recompressing is done.
- Click on Video | Frame Rate or press *Ctrl+R* to bring up the frame-rate dialog.
- In the Source rate adjustment group of settings, select Change to 24 fps as shown below.
- Type in 24 and click OK:

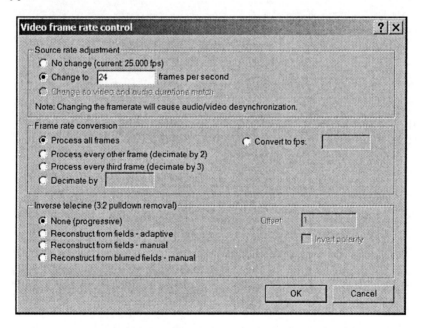

- Press *F7* and save the frame-rate adjusted video. If your video is longer than a couple of minutes, you could select a small portion before saving.

Once you finish the above process, get one of your friends to copy the two files (24 and 25 fps videos) to a new directory and give them random filenames so that you don't know which one is which. Then casually watch both and try guessing which one is faster. Did you succeed?

It is important that you realize that this process has not changed the video content *at all*. You specifically instructed the playback system to play the video at a different rate. In other words, instead of displaying 25 frames per second, it will display 24; this also means the length in frames stays the same, but the duration in time has changed! Verify this by opening the new video in VirtualDub and displaying the File Information dialog. Notice that you can control the frame rate with a precision of up to three decimal places.

Furthermore, if your video had audio parts then the audio and video will appear to be out of synchronization once you change the source frame rate. This is an indication that VirtualDub can only control the rate at which video is being played back! Therefore changing the frame rate is only useful in two cases:

1.   There is no audio and you want to alter the speed of playback.
2.   The audio and video is already out of sync and you are trying to fix that.

In the second case, there are two ways of doing it:

- You can let VirtualDub decide on the frame rate by making sure that audio and video lengths match. This is accomplished by choosing the Change so video and audio durations match option.
- You can manually type the frame rate, as we did earlier, if you know it.

Note that this will only work if the audio is out of synchronization, by varying amounts, throughout the video. There are cases when the audio will playback a constant finite amount of time before or after the video; in other words, you will hear a phrase being spoken a very short amount of time before or after the actor's lips have moved. The "constant" denotes that this will not change throughout the video at all.

However, it is extremely hard to tell which of the two is happening due to the subtleness of these time amounts. For example, in DVDs, it is common for the audio to begin about 80 milliseconds before the video—that is 1/125th of a second!

Therefore, given a video of unknown source, it can be extremely hard to synchronize the audio and video unless it is obvious. If you have been told about the source or why it is out sync you can employ the above process to try to correct it. You will probably encounter a few trial and error cases, especially in the case of offset displacement.

To order VirtualDub to play the audio before or after the video, you need to use the interleaving option that you can access from the Audio | Interleaving menu or by pressing *Ctrl+I*. The following dialog will appear:

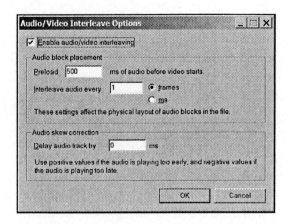

The Audio block placement option is not related to synchronization, but rather to how the chunks of audio are laid out in the file. Changing those settings might help when the audio fails to load quickly enough and there is juttering, but will not help in syncing in any case. The Audio skew correction setting can be used to delay the audio track by a specific amount of time, in milliseconds. If the audio is playing earlier than the video, you can use a positive value to delay it and force it to play along with the video. Conversely, if the audio is playing too late you can use a negative value—this time to make the audio start earlier.

Changing the Actual Frame Rate

Sometimes it is necessary to reduce the actual frame rate of the video, for example when you are going to distribute a lower-resolution version of your video on the World Wide Web. If you reduce the spatial resolution significantly you may as well reduce the temporal resolution (frame rate) by a factor of two or three, depending on your quality requirements. The video will then be easier to encode, it will require less bits, and viewers will have to wait less time to download it.

VirtualDub allows you to reduce the frame rate by an integral factor (N), which is known as "decimating": the effect is accomplished by processing every Nth frame instead of every frame (default action). Decimate does not come in the form of a filter since filters do not add or remove frames from the video! To access the feature, press *Ctrl+R* or select the Video | Frame Rate menu. You may select to decimate by 2, 3 (presets), or another integer that you define in the Decimate by field:

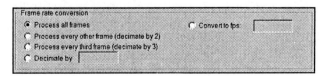

Additionally, it is possible to reduce the frame rate by a non-integral factor; in fact, you can even increase the frame rate! Both of which are possible by defining a custom frame rate in the Convert to fps edit box. VirtualDub will calculate the ratio of source frame rate to destination frame rate as

$$r = \frac{source\ frame\ rate}{destination\ frame\ rate}$$

and duplicate or remove frames as necessary, always attempting to have the closest approximation possible.

Compression affects the down sampling with this method in the same manner as it affects the process of deleting frames; we explained the reasons behind this earlier. If the video is compressed and contains a large number of delta frames, it will not always be possible to remove a frame on demand, since that would break the next delta frame, which depends on it! This is only of concern if we are copying the stream directly to the output (more details on this later). If we are using filters and we have to follow the chain of decompression, filtering, and re-compression there is no such issue—the frames are just skipped. Additionally, if you are up-sampling a compressed source, the additional frames will be "drop frames" (also known as dummy frames). These do not occupy significant amounts of storage; they are commands to repeat the previous frame of the video.

Conversion between PAL and NTSC

If your country uses SECAM for television broadcasts, do not be offended that SECAM is not being mentioned in the title of this section. It is simply because only PAL and NTSC are present in the digital world of video! That is good news because you have to worry about one format less.

I explained earlier why the only *valid* reason to convert from PAL to something lesser like NTSC is if you are forced into it. For example, when you want to burn your AVI file to VideoCD format so that you can play it on your NTSC DVD player (assuming your MPEG-1 encoder does not handle this already). Film material runs at 24 fps and it is converted to 29.970 fps NTSC using a process called 3:2 pulldown. The inelegance of the process comes from the way the additional frames are produced. The original frames are split into interlaced fields of the odd and even lines and those fields are then repeated in a 3:2 pattern. So if we assume four frames from the source labeled A, B, C, D and their corresponding fields A1, A2, B1, B2, C1, C2, D1, D2, the output will be composed of [A1 A2] [A1 B2] [B1 C2] [C1 C2] [D1 D2]—the square brackets denote a frame. Notice:

- There is one more frame in the output for each four frames in the input.
- The first, fourth and fifth frames are progressive (non-interlaced).
- The second and third frames are interlaced.

Repeat this six times and our 24 frames are now 30 seconds each—at a cost. Now the frames are neither all interlaced nor all progressive, but a mixture that would make de-interlacing produce bogus results. On the other hand, we have an extra frame for every four that does not serve any purpose other than to satisfy the NTSC requirements and some of the video is interlaced, resulting in ugly artifacts when there is motion. Luckily, VirtualDub provides the means to reverse the 3:2 pulldown processes, sometimes referred to as inverse telecine. However, there is a catch: it assumes a 3:2 pattern. Other patterns are possible, but most NTSC videos were created with the 3:2 one.

If you possess an NTSC video, open it in VirtualDub and press *Ctrl+R* or select Video | Frame Rate, to invoke the frame-rate control dialog. Select the Reconstruct from fields – adaptive option and press OK. The method is called adaptive because it will detect changes in the way the 3:2 pulldown is made and adapt in order to produce correct results. The manual methods are inferior due to their inability to adapt, and therefore will not work in the majority of cases:

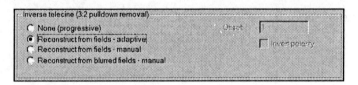

That's it. Your output is now 23.976 fps and if the original was telecined using the 3:2 pattern, then you will now have a nice progressive video with no artifacts: just the way it was meant to be!

Now, if you want to convert to PAL, all you need to do is:

- Adjust the source frame rate to 25 fps.
- Increase the spatial resolution by resizing or adding black bars (see Chapter 6). This is defined by the target format. VideoCD, for example, requires 240 lines for NTSC and 288 lines for PAL.
- Stretch the audio by a factor of 0.958 (-4.2%). We will discuss audio processing in detail later.

You should be a lot more comfortable with the functions of VirtualDub by now.

Converting from PAL to NTSC involves adjusting the frame rate and spatial resolution accordingly. This time, however, changing the source frame rate is not an option since that would involve an approximate increase of 20% in playback speed—something you would most definitely notice. Instead, use the frame-rate conversion feature and VirtualDub will do the job for you; this way you will not need to touch the audio.

Before concluding this section, it is obligatory to insert another reminder: do not convert from one format to another unless there is very good reason, such as removing the artifacts of 3:2 pulldown.

Dealing with Interlaced Sources

Interlacing is another haunting feature of analogue video. It exists for good reason, yet it has several disadvantages. Before we go into the what and the why, let's have a look at a picture with interlacing artifacts so we can examine some of their characteristics:

This enlarged picture that is part of the landscape seems to be unnatural; it looks like alternate lines of pixels have moved towards the right while their counterparts stand still. Don't lose trust in your vision: that is exactly what it is! When a video is interlaced, it is split into fields; a field is simply a set of alternate lines of pixels. Consequently, we have odd- and even- numbered fields in an interlaced frame. The effect you see is because the odd lines are a field from a different progressive (non-interlaced) frame than the even ones (see below). Why would anyone do this to our lovely picture I hear you ask?

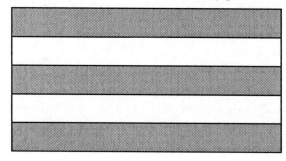

Well, mainly for two reasons and both of them go back to when TV was introduced. The human eye requires moving pictures to refresh at least 50 times per second in order to not notice any flicker. However, when the TV and the related standards were introduced, it was impossible:

1. To have the required bandwidth to transmit 50 frames per second
2. To have the beam inside the TV refresh *all* lines of the picture at that rate

Combine the two and we have interlacing—a way to reduce bandwidth and required refreshing by the monitor.

The assumptions made when the interlacing process was defined are also the reasons why interlaced pictures can look so bad. The TV tuner will receive half-frames, or fields; so on every refresh of the screen (every 1/50 second for PAL) only the odd or even field will be updated. This means that the updated field will be an instant later in time than the one already shown. Therefore, when you're watching TV in a bright environment and particularly when the video shows rapid motion, flicker can be noticed. The phenomenon is even more vivid when the interlaced video is displayed on a progressive device such as a computer CRT monitor since each frame is displayed as a whole (updated every 1/25 seconds in PAL) and the fields don't alternate. If you compare and contrast how the image appears, you will see that on progressive displays it appears as if the two fields are moving together.

For interlaced video, we speak of fields/sec rather than frames/sec because:

- On interlaced devices, a new field is displayed every refresh cycle.
- There is an actual time difference between the two fields displayed at any time. Amateur and older camcorders take advantage of this to capture half-frames on each capture cycle and produce interlaced video. It reduces the processing complexity.

The good news is that there are methods to get rid of interlacing. It costs processing time and the results are not necessarily the desired ones, but it can be done if you have no other choice but to deal with interlaced videos. The specific methods are:

1. Blend odd and even fields
2. Drop odd or even fields
3. Duplicate odd or even fields
4. Field bob

As you might have guessed already, each method has its own advantages and disadvantages, which we are going to explore in the next section.

De-Interlacing Methods

Before I start describing each method, open an interlaced video in VirtualDub—preferably not one that is telecined. Bring up the Filters dialog and add the De-interlace filter; you will observe the following dialog:

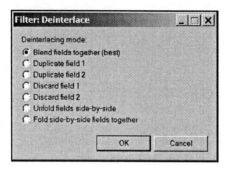

Methods 1 and 2 of the list presented earlier map to the "Duplicate field x" and "Discard field x" options of the VirtualDub de-interlace filter: they are the simplest and quickest ways of de-interlacing, but not necessarily the best ones. Method 2 discards the odd or even field of the image thereby leaving only the other field; the output has half the height of the original. Method 1 is as simple, but this time duplicates the field you specify and therefore preserves the height though not the detail of the image! Of course, the higher the resolution of your video the less image detail you sacrifice, but even if your video resolution is exceptionally high, this is not recommended.

The best the de-interlace filter of VirtualDub can offer is field blending; it blends the two fields together so that the "combing" effect shown at the beginning of this section is not visible any more. However, there might be a "ghosting" side effect during high-motion scenes of the video. Additionally, there is some loss of detail, but in most cases it is less than that caused by discarding or duplicating one of the fields.

The last two options of the de-interlace filter allow you to "fold" or "unfold" the fields of the frame. In simple terms, folding will stack the odd field next to the even field, thus doubling the output's width; unfolding reverses this process. This is particularly useful if you want to apply some filter to the video on a per-field rather than per-frame basis. You consequently avoid blurring of the fields, which would result in ghosting. Naturally, you would then have to fold the fields again in the end.

Field Bob

The last method previously mentioned is "field bob", which is accessible from the corresponding filter in VirtualDub. Bob is different in principle; the two fields of every frame are separated and converted to full frames by resizing the field to twice its height (i.e. equal to the height of the frame).

Thus, there is no field missing from the video output—a benefit that comes at the cost of doubled frame rate. The main drawback of bob is that due to the added frames, processing or playback of the output will require approximately double the computing power. On the other hand, motion will be perfectly fluid in a bob-de-interlaced video.

Since each field is converted into a frame and each frame has two fields, we will have double the number of frames and therefore double the frame rate. Also, after the fields are separated, line 0 of frame 0 will contain the upper field and line 0 of frame 1 will contain the lower field. To correct this overlap that will cause the video to "bob" (it looks as if jumping up and down), we need to push the upper field up and the lower field down!

You might recall that VirtualDub filters do not have the means to insert frames or remove frames from the video—and this would contradict the operation of field bob. Your intuition is right in this case; the field bob filter of VirtualDub will not double the frame rate of the video—it expects a video with fields already split. We will see how that is possible using AviSynth in the next chapter; until then, we will assume we have a video with separated fields as shown in the following image:

Notice that:

- Each field is converted to a frame so we have double the number of frames.
- The frame-rate is doubled and so the duration is kept the same.
- A field is half a frame so the new video has half the vertical resolution of the original.

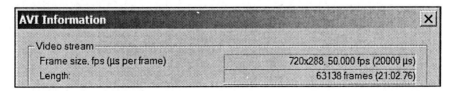

Now, we add the field bob filter as well as a resize filter of our choice to compensate for the reduction of vertical resolution:

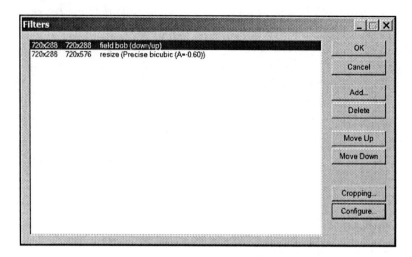

As mentioned above, we need to push the upper field up and the lower field down when applying field bob. Usually the odd field is first and therefore we can configure the filter appropriately as shown in the following screenshot:

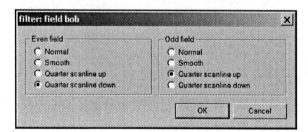

If you do not know which field comes first in your video, preview the output before saving; if you can see the "bob effect" then try swapping the up/down settings.

A quick and dirty way of de-interlacing with field bob is to use the Smooth setting on a normal frame-rate video (i.e. fields are not separated)—this will get rid of the combing. Be aware that there are "smart" de-interlacing filters available at the websites referenced in Chapter 6. They are adaptive to interlacing artifacts and only act upon those areas; they are said to produce even better results than field bob.

Field Swap

There is an extra filter in VirtualDub called **field swap**. As the name suggests, it swaps the fields of each frame. Thus, the odd field replaces the even field and vice versa. Sometimes, progressive video appears to be interlaced because your capture card captured the fields in the wrong order or placed them wrongly in memory. This is not a common case, but field swap will fix it. This filter will not alter the actual video content as it only swaps the pairs of lines.

Hazardous Habits—How to Preserve Quality

In this section we will see how to avoid doing things that will result in a quality loss—errors common to users new to video processing. We will go a little deeper into:

- Converting from one format to another—transcoding
- Lossless and lossy codecs
- Color spaces

Knowing about the above concepts will give you a better understanding of what is going on behind the scenes and allow you to tweak the process.

Re-Compressing Video

Let's think about what happens when re-compressing video. Assume we have a video 'V'. The owner of 'V' used a lossy codec to compress it at a very good quality giving another video 'C'. You are not satisfied with 'C' because it is too grainy for your liking so you open it in VirtualDub, attach a smoother to the filter chain, and save it again.

Saving the video uncompressed would take too much space so we use another, or the same, lossy codec. Throughout, VirtualDub will have to decompress the video, smooth it or apply any other processing you have selected, and finally compress it again with the codec you selected. Now, remember that 'C' is only an *approximation* of 'V' because it was compressed in a *lossy* way.

CRT monitors use three (red, green, blue) electron beams to reproduce the colors of each pixel within the image fed from the computer. Therefore, the **RGB** (Red, Green, and Blue) color space is most natural to them and other display devices. However, it is not the most economical in terms of bandwidth. Since early TV, the YUV color space has been used instead. It consists of an intensity component (Y) and two chroma components (U, V) to represent the colors of the pixels. Properties of human vision are exploited; we are more sensitive to intensity than color. So we can reduce the data needed to represent an image by using one chroma value for 2 or 4 pixels instead of one value for every pixel! This is evident in most, if not all, recent (lossy) video codecs.

So the codec with which 'V' was compressed will give VirtualDub the video in YUV since that's what it uses internally. On the other hand, VirtualDub filters work with RGB since, for most procedures, it makes things easier. As a result, YUV is converted to RGB and the process is lossy.

So far, we had two reductions in quality, firstly because we had to use the approximation of the original video (V) and secondly because YUV had to be converted to RGB ... and we are not finished yet. If you are unsure of why the YUV to RGB conversion is lossy, try the following on a calculator:

$$\boxed{1/3\lrcorner \Rightarrow 0.3333} \text{ but } \boxed{0.3333 \times 3\lrcorner \Rightarrow 0.9999}$$

Floating-point operations are not usually reversible and this error is extended in the YUV conversion because we need to round down to an integer. If you are keen, look for the YUV to RGB matrix and apply a few test values.

After the filtering, RGB is going to be converted back to YUV and then it is going to be compressed again using a lossy method. As you can see, there are many degradations of quality from beginning to end. You might not be able to notice the difference so much if 'V' was of high quality, but if the process is repeated the quality will be lower and lower. In a nutshell, when processing video or sound we can tolerate losses in quality, but it is our duty to try to minimize them as much as possible.

In the above example, if we had used a lossless codec throughout, the only losses would have been absolutely necessary; and converting to RGB to apply the filters and back would depend on the output codec. To conclude, never edit videos compressed in a lossy manner unless you have no other choice.

VirtualDub Processing Modes

The time has come to review the VirtualDub processing modes that can be found under the following Video menu:

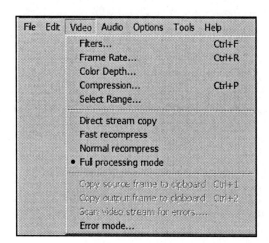

You can select one of the following:

- Direct stream copy
- Fast recompress
- Normal recompress
- Full processing mode

The processing modes aim to provide some benefits at the cost of restricting some of the features of VirtualDub. So when you start editing your video, make sure you select the mode that best suits your needs:

Direct stream copy is self-explanatory: the frames that compose the video stream will be directly copied from the input to the output. Features that would alter the frame content are disabled, for example, filters, depth control, and compression, but not frame-rate options and cut/copy/paste. Use direct stream copy if the source is compressed and you are only shuffling things around.

Fast recompress does not allow any color space conversion to occur and so filters and depth-control menus are disabled. It is a very useful feature that makes sure unnecessary calculations are not performed that also reduce quality and speed of processing. **Normal recompress** is similar in nature, but allows you to control the depth of color. Use Full processing mode if you want to apply filters.

Full processing mode does not set any restrictions and therefore it's the only mode where filters can be used. A roundtrip to RGB is in this case necessary; note that as of version 1.6.0 of VirtualDub, the roundtrip is avoided when no filtering is performed. However you should use fast recompress if you want to recompress without applying any filters; fast recompress also gives priority to YUV color spaces in contrast to the auto-detect default setting of full processing mode.

Recovering Damaged Files

Quite a few times, I have been unable to play back a video file from an old, scratched CD I archived a long time ago. This happens just as often with files downloaded over unreliable networks. The real problem in these cases lies in identifying where the problem is, and fixing it, if possible. Don't worry, VirtualDub supplies all the tools to aid recovery and they are very sophisticated internally, probably more than those of other commercial and pricey video-processing applications.

The source of the problem is usually either that the index of the video file is missing or broken or that some of the frames cannot be decoded. Every AVI file contains an index with vital information about each frame (such as whether it is a key frame). The index is placed at the end of the file and therefore data losses at that part will be fatal; an AVI file cannot be successfully played without an index.

However, VirtualDub can rebuild the index for us in some cases. Secondly, some of the frames might have suffered data losses as well. In the best-case scenario, this will mean those individual frames will not be displayed or they will be displayed, but crippled. In the worst case, the damage will prevent the next frames from being displayed (for example when a key frame is in error).

If you open a video with damaged index in VirtualDub, the program will attempt to parse the file without the index as shown in the following figure:

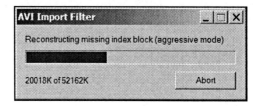

The process might take a while depending on how badly damaged and how long the video is. At the end of the process, a summary will appear like the one shown in the following figure:

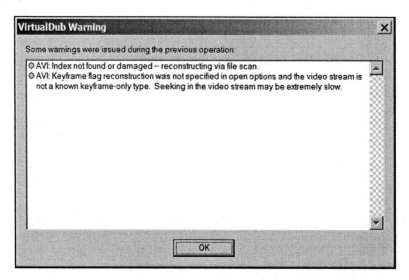

As the warning says, seeking is bound to be very slow when the index is missing because VirtualDub will need to decode all the frames from the beginning to the point you seek to! To fix the file, we need to re-open it and this time order VirtualDub to re-derive the key-frame flags so we can save the file with a proper index.

To achieve this, select File | Open video file; when the dialog pops up, select the damaged file. Also tick the Ask for extended options after this dialog box. Finally, click on Open and the following dialog will be displayed:

Click on the Re-derive keyframe flags option and then on OK. VirtualDub will construct the missing index and re-key the frames. Now, select Video | Direct Stream Copy to disallow any processing and save it to a different file—it should now play correctly.

Another useful feature for errors is the Video | Scan video stream. As the name suggests it scans the stream for bad frames and lets you know not only how many frames have been damaged, but also how many frames cannot be decoded, but are not damaged. As noted earlier this might happen with damaged key frames.

If you find this intriguing but have no files to test it with, open a file with your hex editor and employ a destructive behavior. The hex editor bundled with VirtualDub (Tools | Hex editor) is read-only, but the RIFF chunk tree (Edit | RIFF chunk tree) can be very useful as it identifies the ranges of each frame and the index.

Finally, note that when downloading video files from the Internet, some of them have been mistakenly given the wrong extension. Files with extension .avi are not always true AVI files. VirtualDub can help you identify AVI and MPEG-1 files! Simply open them in VirtualDub and if there is something wrong with them, VirtualDub will let you know about it.

Manually Controlling Input/Output Colorspaces

VirtualDub is a very reliable and robust application and it is safe to trust VirtualDub more than your codec provider, especially for some older codecs. As of VirtualDub 1.6.0, you can control the colorspace request from the decompressor as well as the colorspace fed into the compressor.

Normally you do not need to worry about these settings, but in some cases you might want to force the codec into one particular setting so that VirtualDub can do the rest. Bring up the configuration (shown below) via Video | Color Depth; the left column controls the format that VirtualDub will request *from* the codec, while the right column controls the format that VirtualDub will deliver *to* the codec:

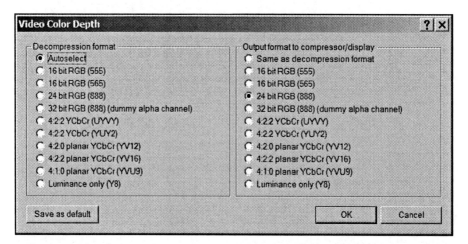

A popular example is chroma interpolation; most codecs that compress in YUV have reduced resolution of U and V and do not fully interpolate when decompressing. Using this feature, you could force the codec to output its native color space so that VirtualDub can do the up sampling. To do this, you need to have this information, which is not available in all cases.

Summary

Chapter 8 rounds up the features of VirtualDub related to video-specific processing. We discussed:

- Why the different video formats/standards like PAL and NTSC exist and their relative properties
- How to identify the video format of a particular video

- How to distinguish between the playback rate of a video and the actual frame rate and how to alter either of these
- How interlacing works and how to visually identify it, as well as methods of removing the artifacts it introduces when played back on progressive displays
- The importance of calculations in video and how to minimize the degradation of video evident when processing and compressing video
- How to fix broken video files
- How to override the (de)compression color space to circumvent bugs in codecs

You should congratulate yourself for making it this far; some of the concepts introduced in this chapter are quite technical and difficult to understand!

9

Frameserving

Frameserving is the simple concept of serving, passing, and feeding uncompressed frames to another application. For instance, if you have a video-processing application (it can even be a player) that cannot decode MPEG-1 files, you can use a **frameserver** to copy the frames from an MPEG-1 file to the application. This is usually done by writing a small dummy file that contains data specific to the frameserver, but is visible as a large uncompressed file to other applications. Most frameservers available can also process the video before passing it to the next application down the chain.

In this chapter, we will explore two frameservers—the one provided with VirtualDub and a second one called AviSynth. By the end of the chapter, you will know:

- How to install and serve frames from MPEG-1 or AVI files through the VirtualDub frameserver
- How to use AviSynth to serve frames from any file format your computer can decode, to any application (including VirtualDub)
- How to use AviSynth to apply filters

What is AviSynth?

AviSynth is a free, open source frameserver: it will serve frames to any application that uses the Video for Windows or DirectShow interfaces. Like VirtualDub, AviSynth has a modular structure that allows the use of plug-ins; in fact, you can load VirtualDub filters in AviSynth! So why opt for it?

Well, the first versions of AviSynth were only able to open AVI files, but it has matured over the years and is now able to open any media file supported by DirectShow, and there are plug-ins for many file formats such as MPEG-2. Furthermore, the open source community has contributed to the adoption of AviSynth with the development of plug-ins for all sorts of uses, from de-interlacing to quality assessment. On the other hand, AviSynth is not as easy to use as VirtualDub; it incorporates a scripting language versus the intuitive graphical user interface of VirtualDub. In short, the main reasons to use AviSynth over VirtualDub are:

- To process a video format that is not supported by VirtualDub
- To use a filter that is only available for AviSynth

It is a skill in life to use the right tool for the right job!

What Frameservers Can Do

The VirtualDub frameserver supports:

- VirtualDub video filters
- Audio displacement/skew correction
- Audio source multiplexing
- Range editing (such as selection and deletion)

Unsupported features are:

- Inverse telecine (3:2 pulldown removal)
- Audio conversion and interleaving
- Compression—both for video and audio
- Filters that introduce a lag (e.g. temporal smoother)

The above list gives you a good idea of what is possible with the VirtualDub frameserver. AviSynth is very extensive due to the high number of plug-ins available out there; with respect to VirtualDub, it isn't so much what you can do but what you *cannot* do with it, for example:

- Capturing video
- Audio and video multiplexing
- Video or audio compressing
- Range editing

The list is not exhaustive and I should point out that a frameserver is very different in nature to VirtualDub itself: It will deliver uncompressed frames to the target application. Therefore compressing is fundamentally impossible. This also renders multiplexing and range editing inefficient since direct stream copy is not possible, and this would be required to re-compress the output. Note that there is nothing to stop you chaining more than one frameserver and taking advantage of the features of each of them!

By the end of this chapter, you will feel more comfortable with the notion, so do not worry if things are a little vague right now.

Setting Up the VirtualDub Frameserver

Both AviSynth and the VirtualDub frameserver are very easy to set up. For VirtualDub:

- Locate auxsetup.exe in the directory where VirtualDub lies.
- Double-click on auxsetup.exe.
- Click on Install handler. The following dialog will pop up.
- Click OK.
- VirtualDub will let you know if the installation was successful or not:

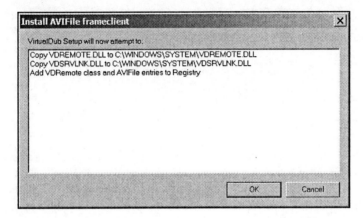

If you later want to remove the frameserver for any reason, you can click on Uninstall handler. Press Exit to exit the utility.

The frameserver works by writing a file with the .vdr extension. Whenever you open the file with another application, VirtualDub will process the frames and then pass them on. Some applications will attempt to force an .avi extension while opening files and are therefore unable to receive frames from the VirtualDub frameserver.

For this reason, VirtualDub also features a proxy mode. When in proxy mode, the VirtualDub frameserver will be placed on top of the AVI handler of Windows. When frames from an AVI file are requested, the requests will be passed on to the AVI handler. In the case of a .vdr file renamed to .avi, VirtualDub will handle the serving.

However, because of this pass-through attribute of the proxy, some applications may malfunction when the VirtualDub frameserver is in proxy mode, so enable proxy mode only when needed. To enable proxy mode, locate the aviproxy directory in the VirtualDub installation and double-click on proxyon.reg. To disable, double-click on proxyoff.reg.

Serving Frames with VirtualDub

Launch VirtualDub and open an AVI file of your choice; we will serve its frames to another instance of VirtualDub so you may add a few filters if you like. Of course, serving frames between two VirtualDub instances is of no particular use, but it demonstrates the concept. There is an incompatibility of the frameserver with DirectShow and so you cannot use it with most recent video players. The application you will be serving frames to strictly needs to be using the older Video for Windows interface. AviSynth, on the other hand, can serve frames to any application since it supports DirectShow.

After you finish setting up VirtualDub, click on File | Start Frameserver. The following dialog will appear:

This allows you to set a name for the frameserver; BENT is the network name of my computer set in Windows. The second part designates the name of the file served and you can change it to whatever you like. Press Start and save the .vdr file that corresponds to the frameserver. A dialog with some statistics on the frameserver will appear.

Now, launch another instance of VirtualDub (yes, you can have as many as you like!) and click on File | Open. Locate the .vdr file you previously saved and click Open. You should now be able to see the processed video served from the first instance of VirtualDub in the second instance! Also, the statistics dialog of the first instance should have updated as shown in the following dialog—the numbers may vary:

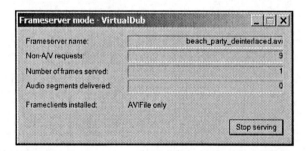

Notice that the frameserver acts just like a normal video file; you can seek, play, etc. This sums up the VirtualDub frameserver; we will now go into AviSynth briefly.

Setting Up AviSynth

AviSynth is available free from its homepage at http://www.avisynth.org/, where you can also find the full documentation and additional filters!

To set up AviSynth:

- Follow the download link at its homepage to SourceForge.

- Locate the AviSynth 2.5 download group and click on the most recent entry with the .exe (executable) extension. That will redirect you to a list of mirrors from which you can select one near you. Be careful not to download an alpha version as those are only available for testing purposes and are likely to be unstable.

- Once the download is done, double-click on the file and follow the simple instructions to install it. That's it!

Before we serve frames with AviSynth, we need to familiarize ourselves with the scripting language it employs. No previous experience with scripting is required, but if you have any you will find it trivial.

Introduction to AviSynth Scripts

Launch Notepad or your favorite text editor and type the following text:

```
# My first script
Version()
```

Save the file as version.avs and drag-and-drop it to a video player of your choice—e.g. Windows Media Player. You should see a 10 seconds long video with the version information of AviSynth (sample shown below). The text that follows the # above, is treated as a comment:

AviSynth 2.55, build:Jul 15 2004 [16:39:25]
© 2000-2004 Ben Rudiak-Gould, et al.
http://www.avisynth.org

That was simple, wasn't it? version() is a built-in function of AviSynth and there are many others to suit every purpose. For those unfamiliar with scripting, you may invoke a function by typing its function name followed by round brackets (parentheses) to designate the function call. In the above case, the function did not require any parameters or arguments; otherwise, we would need to specify them within the round brackets.

For example, let us load an AVI file and serve it to our video player with the following script:

```
AVISource("d:\path\to\my_file.avi")
```

If you open this script in your video player or even VirtualDub, you should be able to see the contents of my_file.avi. AviSynth 2.5 and later, uses the YV12 color space as output by default—a variant of YUV. If your application fails to load the script, you can use either ConvertToYUY2 or ConvertToRGB to export a friendlier format:

```
AVISource("d:\path\to\my_file.avi")
ConvertToRGB()
```

Notice that we put the name of the file within the brackets, surrounded by double quotes as AVISource() requires the name of the file to open. This is because the filename is a string literal; we will see the difference with variable and number arguments shortly. If you had multiple parameters, you would have to separate them with a comma, like:

```
function_name(arg1, arg2, …, argN)
```

If you have a background in programming languages, you will notice that ending the line with a semicolon produces a syntactical error. You can find reference notes on all built-in filters at http://www.avisynth.org/index.php?page=AviSynthManual.

This gives us a very good introduction to AviSynth—enough to proceed with frameserving. In fact, we have already done that in the previous example!

Variables

Sometimes variables are useful in our AviSynth scripts, especially when we are dealing with multiple videos. For example, the script

```
AVISource("d:\path\to\my_file.avi")
```

is equivalent to

```
my_file = AVISource("d:\path\to\my_file.avi")
…
return my_file
```

The AVISource() function will, by default, return the video included in the file. In the above script, we are assigning the my_file variable to the return value of AVISource() so we can later refer to it through my_file. At the bottom of the script, we are returning my_file to designate the output of this script.

In the same way, we could have assigned the filename to another variable my_file_name:

```
my_file_name = "d:\path\to\my_file.avi"
my_file = AVISource(my_file_name)
…
return my_file
```

This would have worked in the same way as above.

The same goes for numbers; the `AssumeFps()` function is used to change the playback rate of the video:

```
my_file_name = "d:\path\to\my_file.avi"
target_fps = 12.5
my_file = AVISource(my_file_name)
my_file = AssumeFps(my_file, target_fps)
...
return my_file
```

Source Filter and Supported Formats

The greatest advantage of AviSynth over VirtualDub is its ability to read multiple file and video formats, using third-party plug-ins. This expands the possibilities beyond AVI files; in fact, AviSynth has a built-in source filter that utilizes DirectShow and thus allows you to import any format that can be played through DirectShow. The requirement for DirectShow playback is the existence of source, de-multiplexing, and decoder filters for the particular format. DVDs for example, are encoded in the MPEG-2 format and modern DVD playback applications like WinDVD and PowerDVD (usually one of them is bundled with retail DVD-readers) provide the necessary filters.

To open a file through DirectShow, you need to employ `DirectShowSource` as shown in the following script:

```
DirectShowSource("my_mpeg4_file.mp4")
```

Assuming that your system has filters registered for MPEG-4 playback, AviSynth will serve the video to any application, including VirtualDub. If on the other hand, there are no filters available that will produce valid AviSynth output when playing back the script, you will get the error message The Filter Graph won't talk to me. When that happens you need to install a suitable DirectShow decoder.

Due to some DirectShow quirks, you might need to specify the frame rate of the video and whether seeking is possible, like this:

```
DirectShowSource("my_mpeg4_file.mp4", 25.0, false)
```

The value `false` (last parameter) designates that there are no seeking abilities.

Loading Third-Party Plug-ins in AviSynth

As mentioned previously, it is possible to load external plug-ins in a fashion similar to VirtualDub. AviSynth filters come with the `.dll` extension and you can find a non-exhaustive list at http://www.avisynth.org/warpenterprises/. To load a plug-in, you need to use the `LoadPlugin` function:

```
LoadPlugin("d:\path\to\plugin.dll")
# I can now use functions imported by the plug-in
```

If you use a plug-in regularly and want to avoid loading it manually every time, you could place it in the plugins subdirectory of the AviSynth installation.

Previously, it was stated that it is possible to load and use VirtualDub filters in AviSynth; it is, however, somewhat obscure to do that yourself. Fortunately, the AviSynth community has created a set of functions that simplifies the process of loading and using some common VirtualDub filters! On the other hand, it is not possible to use any of the built-in default filters shipped with VirtualDub. For more information see http://www.avisynth.org/ShareFunctions/; if the filter you would like to use is not in the list and you want to implement a function yourself, see section 4 of the AviSynth FAQ at http://www.avisynth.org/AviSynthFaq/. You will find however that most, if not all, VirtualDub filters have an equivalent in AviSynth that can save you the trouble.

Separating the Fields of an Interlaced Video

In the previous chapter, I promised I would show you how to separate the fields of an interlaced video so that you can apply bob. Thanks for your patience: the following few lines will fulfil that promise. AviSynth contains a built-in function SeparateFields(), which does exactly what we want. In order to serve the fields of a file into VirtualDub, the following script is sufficient:

```
AVISource("d:\path\to\my_file.avi")
SeparateFields()
```

You can control which field will compose the first frame in the output using the ComplementParity() function. By default, the bottom field is output first; the following script will output the top field first:

```
AVISource("d:\path\to\my_file.avi")
ComplementParity()
SeparateFields()
```

Summary

We are now one more step up the ladder of video processing. As you can see, frameserving can prove to be very useful because:

- You can serve AVI and MPEG-1 files through VirtualDub alone—no additional software is required. At the same time, you can apply filters and multiplex audio and video.

- Older applications that use the Video for Windows interface can now read any file via a DirectShow tunnel in AviSynth.

- You now have access to a huge library of additional filters you can use through AviSynth.

We touched on the significance of using the right tool for the right job and this chapter aimed to help you realize the potential of both frameservers so that you may take the right decision in the face of future problems. You will find that using VirtualDub is convenient most of the time since it can compress the output. AviSynth on the other hand is useful to accomplish tasks VirtualDub cannot carry out. One does need to think of the two applications as separate; you could serve frames with AviSynth to VirtualDub and use the latter to do the filtering and compressing. The aim is to minimize the processing.

10

Compressing: A World of Codecs

We have used the term 'codec' quite a lot in earlier chapters without defining what it means. A **codec** is just a *co*mpression and *dec*ompression engine. It does not refer only to digital video, but also to audio and other forms of data. However, in this book, we are only concerned with video and audio codecs.

Previously, we classified codecs as lossless and lossy. This classification is only evident for audio and video codecs. Data compression does not tolerate data losses, so all data codecs are lossless. Imagine compressing a very important archive of documents only to find they are corrupted when you decompress them! You probably do not want that to happen with your video or audio. Lossy video codecs exploit redundancies in the video frames and insensitivities of the human visual system to reduce the amount of data required to represent the original video.

Audio codecs take advantage of properties of the human auditory system, striving to squeeze the bits of the audio stream. Of course, this process is irreversible. By definition, the compressed data cannot be re-constructed to be identical to the source. The aim is to make this process as accurate as possible and thereby produce the best approximation! In technical terms, lossy codecs (given the constraints of bit-rate and distortion) attempt to minimize the error between the original and decompressed streams.

Microsoft Windows has several video and audio codecs installed by default, but most of them are somewhat deprecated and out of date. On the other hand, there are numerous other commercial and free codecs and most are accessible from the Internet. Obviously, people with limited budgets would prefer the free to the commercial ones, and most companies are starting to realize that the end user cannot spend a vast amount of money to encode a video every now and then.

The decoders for the codecs are normally offered free so that anyone can watch a video encoded with a given codec, even if it is commercial.

In this section we present some of the codecs compatible with VirtualDub. There are several others, but their description is out of the scope of this book. We will compare them at the conceptual rather than the implementation level because:

1. The relative merits of visual and audio quality are entirely subjective.
2. The quality of a particular implementation often changes from version to version.

Often, evaluation versions of codecs are offered and if you are keen in keeping up-to-date, you can check the online reviews and community discussions. Always perform your own tests because what might work for someone else might not work for you and vice versa. The following tables provide information on a few popular codecs:

Video codecs

Name	Type	Location
HuffYUV	Free / Lossless	http://neuron2.net/www.math.berkeley.edu/benrg/huffyuv.html
DivX	Commercial / Lossy	http://www.divx.com/
XviD	Free / Lossy	http://www.xvid.org/
3ivX	Commercial / Lossy	http://www.3vix.com/
Morgan MJPEG	Commercial / Lossy	http://www.morgan-multimedia.com/
Pegasus Imaging MJPEG	Commercial / Lossy	http://www.pegasusimaging.com/
On2 VP6	Commercial / Lossy	http://www.on2.com/

Audio codecs

Name	Type	Location
LAME MP3	Free / Lossy	http://mitiok.free.fr/
FhG IIS MP3	Commercial / Lossy	Official website is http://www.iis.fraunhofer.de/, but it is not distributed any more
Speex	Free / Lossy	http://www.openacm.org/

Vendors such as Microsoft and Real Networks provide their own codecs, but they are not compatible with VirtualDub and therefore not described in this book.

You should not expect lossless codecs to achieve very high compression ratios; certainly not as high as lossy codecs. On the video side, HuffYUV has established a large user-base over the years since it is very stable; it is based on the Huffman tables utilized in many data compression formats as well.

You must have noticed that there are two Motion JPEG (MJPEG) codecs in the above table. Although lossy, this family of codecs provides good quality at low compression ratios as each frame is coded independently and errors do not accumulate. The compression algorithm is based on the popular JPEG image compression standard.

The third family of codecs in the above table is based on the MPEG-4 video-coding standard—DivX, XviD, and 3ivX. The similarity of names is due to their parent—OpenDivX; all three inherit from the latter in one way or another. This family offers very good lossy compression with good quality at high compression ratios.

Last but not the least, there is On2's VP6—a proprietary technology that is not based on any known standard methods. This does not mean that VP6 is necessarily inferior to other codecs that use standard methods; interoperability, however, is unavailable.

There are fewer choices on the audio side. As with video codecs, the interfaces offered by Windows and supported by VirtualDub have become very limited and tedious to use. Most vendors have moved on to the new DirectShow platform, which has more capabilities. The two codecs available at the time of authoring are LAME and Speex.

- **LAME** is an MP3 encoder, compatible with almost every device having playback capabilities.
- **Speex** is a proprietary format that is largely used for speech encodings; it provides good compression ratios for speech at a good quality, but does not perform well for music.

There is a commercial MP3 codec made by Fraunhofer (FhG), but you will only be able to find it at locations other than the official website. Last but not the least, there is an Ogg Vorbis codec compatible with VirtualDub, but it has not been updated for quite some time and is therefore not recommended.

Most vendors tend to provide playback software for a few platforms (Windows, Linux, Macintosh, etc.). These change from time to time so do check each vendor's website to see if your target platform is supported. Open standards disassociate a technology from any one particular vendor and give more freedom to the end user; we will go into more detail on compatibility and open standards in the following section.

Interoperability and Open Standards

Interoperability is a very controversial subject, with many keen fanatics on both sides of the issue. It can be defined as the ability to exchange and use information. How does this apply to the world of computers? Consider DVDs as an example: once you buy a film on DVD, you can play it back on your computer, portable/set-top DVD player, and nowadays in your car! All those devices, even though they are different, can read and understand the DVD format. This is because DVD is based on MPEG-2—a standard developed over many years of research by video experts from many companies and organizations.

MPEG-2 aimed for high quality and high bit-rate applications and therefore has limited scalability. Mediums having lower capacity (e.g. networks or digital discs) are unable to use MPEG-2 effectively. The next video standard—MPEG-4, was developed with scalability in mind and so many more devices are able to decode MPEG-4-compliant streams. This includes all of the devices mentioned earlier, as well as cell phones, PDAs, and any other device with reasonable processing abilities! MPEG is a body that defines open standards; any company or individual can access the standards for a fee. More and more companies thus get involved and the end user enjoys a larger variety of products. An MPEG-4-compliant video stream should be decodable by *any* compliant decoder of the same or higher processing capabilities—be it software or hardware. The controversy lies in the fact that patent fees support the development costs of the standard for commercial applications.

These characteristics guarantee a much greater chance of being able to transfer your videos from one device to the other, but they do not guarantee a higher quality than their rivals do. It is yet another case of using the right tool for the right job; if you are concerned about who is going to be able to play back your video then you should pick the codec that uses the standard with the appropriate interoperability attributes. On the other hand, if you are most concerned about the perceived quality and you can safely assume all the viewers will possess the corresponding decoder then you should use the codec you visually like the most, even if it is based on a proprietary technology.

However, even if you use any of the MPEG-4 codecs listed above to encode your video, you cannot play it back on any MPEG-4 compliant device. Although your video will be encoded in a supported format, your audio might not be (MP3 should be OK). Even if it is, the file format will be different from that of MPEG-4. In other words, the device will need to be able to parse the AVI file format, but there are ways and free applications to convert an AVI file to native MPEG-4 file (e.g. MP4 UI from `http://mp4ui.sourceforge.net/`). It is best to follow the latter method as MPEG-4 AVI players might restrict the accepted codecs to one particular vendor.

Older Codecs

Windows ships with several codecs that VirtualDub may use. Launch VirtualDub to see what options are available to you. Select Video | Compression (the associated keyboard shortcut has changed in version 1.6.0 from *Ctrl+C* to *Ctrl+P)*:

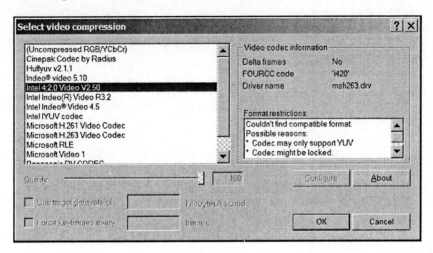

The list is populated with all the codecs available to VirtualDub. When you select one, VirtualDub will also display any known restrictions such as accepted color spaces on the right. In all honesty, the only codecs that you might ever use from that list are Microsoft's H.261 and H.263 codecs. H.261 was designed for video-conferencing applications at bit rates that are multiples of 64 kilobits per second. H.263 advanced on H.261 resulting in higher coding efficiency. Unfortunately, both of them are locked and you cannot use them to compress video! Do not sigh; they are not exactly state-of-the-art anyway!

The same applies to audio codecs; the one that ships with Windows does not permit high-quality encodings. In particular, the MP3 codec bundle allows encodings of up to 56kbps at 24 kHz. At those bit-rates, the MP3 standard cannot perform well enough for archiving video; it might be suitable for low-quality Internet video. To check the list of codecs, select Audio | Full Processing Mode and then Audio | Compression. The resulting dialog will look like the following screenshot:

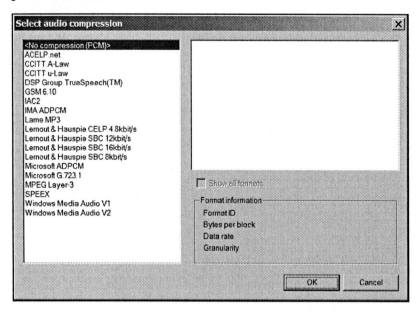

You can see the two extra codecs (LAME and Speex) that I have installed; we will learn how to install them in the next section.

Adding Codecs

Before you go ahead and buy any of the listed commercial codecs, you should try their evaluation versions and compare them with the free ones. Most vendors allow 30 days of encoding time or a limited number of encodings, so you should be able to encode a few of your videos. If you are not satisfied with the output or you feel that the free codecs serve you better, go with your instinct—there is nothing to guarantee that commercial software will be better than free software! A lot of the time, free software gives highly priced software a hard run for money: VirtualDub is a perfect example—it's the king of video-processing applications in its range.

Codecs will often come with an installer, in which case installation is trivial. Double-click on the executable and follow the instructions. Others will come in a ZIP file, which you need to extract; they will also contain a file with the .inf extension. Right-click on the file and select Install—everything else will be taken care of for you.

The tables in the previous section are only a starting point showing the most popular codecs available. When you get involved with the multimedia community, you will find out about less popular and possibly experimental codecs you might want to try. It will take a few trials and errors for you to find the codec most suitable to your needs and most pleasant to your eyes.

Compressing Video

This section will guide you through the steps of compressing video using the basic settings. You will also be introduced to some of the concepts used in modern codecs (such as DivX) so that you are better equipped to configure those to your needs. We will also touch on the issues of interoperability we mentioned earlier, but this time on a lower and more specific level.

The public interface that the operating system exposes to applications like VirtualDub is Video for Windows. This offers a simplistic way of defining the codec options before you encode a video. That is, it allows you to specify:

- A quality factor (0 to 100)
- The data rate in kilobytes/sec
- The maximum interval that the stream will not contain a key-frame

There are two important points to note here:

1. The data rate is specified in *kilobytes* instead of *kilobits*; kilobits are a measure commonly used in the world of lossy compression.
2. The key-frame interval is very important as it will define how precisely you will be able to seek in the file.

If you don't understand why, let me remind you that key-frames are the points in the video stream that the codec can decompress independently without decompressing any other frames. However, this interface is supported by very few codecs (even some of the default codecs do not support this), simply because the configuration is complex. That does not mean it is hard to configure modern codecs; we will go through some points common in current technologies. Remember that even if you find a codec not described here, the defaults tend to work fine for the average user.

Let's look at this interface so that you know how to use it. Launch VirtualDub, open your favorite video and select Video | Compression (*Ctrl+P*). At the bottom left of the dialog you will see the controls shown in the following screenshot:

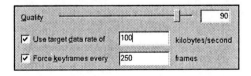

Usually the data rate will be preferred over the quality setting as it might be necessary to impair the video to adhere to the target data rate. Of course, these depend on the particular codec and its internal workings—if you are unsure, consult the help pages of the codec's manufacturer.

The data rate is in *kilobytes* (*kilobits* are used throughout the book) so you will need to divide the number of kilobits you want to spend each second by 8—since each byte consists of 8 bits. We will get to the bit-rate calculation shortly.

It is also a common and good practice to limit the number of non-key frames to ten seconds worth of video, since it provides a good compromise between compressions and seekability.

Once you have set the three variables to your liking, select a codec and you are ready to start the compression. Just press OK.

Saving the Video

To save the video, simply select Video | Save as AVI or press *F7*. The familiar Save As dialog will pop up and ask you to specify a filename. Once you type in the name and specify the path click Save; VirtualDub will now process and compress the file you opened using the filter chain and compression settings you've defined. The following Progress window will pop up:

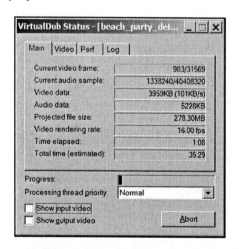

The dialog contains some very useful information about the process in progress. The Projected file size is an estimation of the final file size, but do not sweat if it's under or above your expectations. This is a very rough estimation and it depends on how many bytes the codec spent in recent frames. Most modern codecs utilize intelligent rate control algorithms that will try to keep the average data rate to the number you have specified. They are able to distribute more bits to complex frames and fewer bits to simple ones. The same applies to the estimated total time; the encoding time of each frame will vary and so it is hard to estimate the total time accurately.

Note that it is useful to change the thread priority to a lower level if you are working on your computer and simultaneously encoding with VirtualDub—selecting Normal will often cause the computer to stall. If you close this window without clicking on Abort, VirtualDub will continue its task. Furthermore, you will notice that the menus of VirtualDub are changed while processing. If you wish to make the window reappear select Options | Show Status Window. To abort the operation, select File | Abort dub.

Job Control

Job control is a particularly useful feature when you wish to run multiple tasks in series. If intensive computing is part of your job, it is often annoying to encode as you work; it slows down the process awfully and sometimes stalls the computer, interrupting your work and causing frustration. Using job control you can queue several tasks at any point in time and then command VirtualDub to run them later.

To add a task to the job queue:

- Open your desired video.
- Add the filters, if any.
- Select processing mode.
- Select codec and configuration options.
- Click Save As and check the Don't run this job now; add it to job control so I can run it in batch mode box.
- Click Save.

Nothing will happen now; the job is already queued and waiting for you to run it. You can access Job Control via File | Job Control or by pressing *F4*:

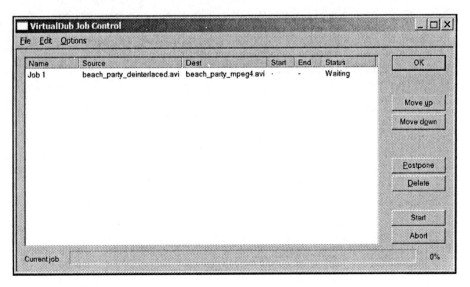

The dialog has the necessary controls (Move up, Move down) to order the processing and Postpone, Delete, Start, or Abort for the execution. A postponed job will not be executed; so once you start running the jobs, you cannot pause the current job and resume it later.

Another handy feature that VirtualDub's job control provides is to shutdown the computer when all the jobs are finished—you can see this in the Options menu. You can also save/load job lists from the File menu.

Calculating the Video and Audio Bitrate

This will involve a few lines of trivial mathematical calculations and it merely depends on the purpose of the encoded video. For example, you will use different bitrates for the video on your website and a CD version. We will see how to calculate the bitrate in both circumstances. We are mainly concerned with the video, as it will take up most of the space of the file, but we will also take audio into account.

It is obvious that the audio and video bitrate added together equal the total bitrate:

$$b_{audio} + b_{video} = b_{total}$$

The total bitrate will depend on whether the medium is the Internet or a CD. The balance between audio and video bitrate depends on the content of the movie; you would spend more bits for the audio clip of a music video than for the audio clip of a conference video recording. This is justified because speech contains lower frequencies than music and is therefore easier to compress efficiently. The following table provides a list of bitrates normally used for encoding different kinds of content on different mediums. Audio bitrates are based on the LAME MP3 encoder and for Internet transmissions, video dimensions are downsized.

Audio/Video	Content Type	Medium	Bitrate
Audio	Speech	Disc	64-128kbps
Audio	Speech	Internet	32-64kbps
Audio	Music	Disc	192-320kbps
Audio	Music	Internet	96-192kbps
Audio	Dialogue & Music (Movie)	Disc	128-320kbps
Audio	Dialogue & Music (Movie)	Internet	64-160kbps
Video	Low motion (Conference/News)	Internet	200-400kbps
Video	Mix of low & high motion	Internet	600-1200kbps

These values are only an indication to get you started. As you gain experience, you will learn to take into account the target audience, target medium, and their capabilities (lower bitrates for slower Internet connections, and vice versa).

You might have noticed that we limit the audio bitrate more than the video range; the reason is that video occupies most of the allocated bits and we usually adjust the video bitrate with respect to the audio bitrate and total number of bits available. To understand this more clearly, we'll work through an example.

For medium-to-high video resolutions you will be able to fit anywhere from 60 to 120 minutes worth of video and audio on a single 80min (700MB) CD-R disc. Let's assume that the duration of a movie is 90 minutes:

- Calculate the number of seconds: $90 \times 60 = 5400 \ seconds$

- Calculate the total number of bytes available:

  $700 \times 1024 = 716800 kbytes \times 1024 = 734003200 bytes$

- First choose the desired audio bitrate e.g. 128 $kbps$

- Calculate the number of bytes needed for the audio:

  $$\frac{128}{8} KBps \times 5400 = 86400 kbytes \times 1024 = 88473600 bytes$$

- Calculate the number of bytes available for the video:
  $734003200 - 88473600 = 645529600 \ bytes$

- Calculate the number of bytes available for each second of video:
  $$\frac{645529600}{5400} = 119542 bytes$$

- Calculate the video bitrate: $\frac{119542}{1024} \times 8 = 934 \ kbps$

First we calculate the total number of bytes available, i.e. 700MB. (Most of the time we should subtract about 5-10MB from the real size of the disc to allow for the AVI overheads and overshoots of the encoders.) Then we choose the audio bitrate, mainly for two reasons:

- Audio is relatively easier to encode and we therefore know what bitrate will sound good to our ears.

- Audio encoders are usually more accurate than video encoders are.

Having chosen the bitrate we can calculate the space required for the audio of our movie. Consequently, we calculate the available number of bytes for the video and the video bitrate. The multiplications and divisions by 8 convert from bytes to bits and vice versa.

If you feel that these calculations are too much work for each of your videos, you may find a bitrate calculator useful—you will find several on the Internet.

Variable, Average, and Constant Bitrate Modes

Most modern and sophisticated codecs (video and audio) have several encoding modes:

- **Average bitrate (ABR):** The encoder will try to match the bitrate specified, but it is free to distribute the available bits unevenly to each frame. In other words, it is given the freedom to spend more bits for complex frames or scenes and fewer for simpler ones.

- **Variable bitrate (VBR):** The encoder will encode the video at a given quality and not try to limit the bitrate. The quality is usually given as a percentage or as a **quantizer** for MPEG and similar video codecs.

- **Constant bitrate (CBR):** The encoder is bound to spend a specific number of bits for each frame. In some cases, this works as the upper limit; the encoder is free to spend as many bits as necessary, but no more than the specified bitrate. This mode has application in networks and is not offered by many video encoders.

In case you are not familiar with the concept, a quantizer is a number that maps a range of values. Intuitively, it controls the accuracy of the codec; lower quantizers will produce higher quality video. Often, the VBR mode is offered via quantizers; the encoding process will not vary for each frame. However, it is important to note that fixed quantizer implies constant bitrate! Although the quantizer controls how much data will be discarded for each frame, the actual output will vary depending on the frame content.

Multi-Pass Encoding

Multi-pass encoding is an essential feature, which is relatively simple in principle. Two-pass encoding is very common although not all encoders will incorporate this.

Multi-pass encoding is a technique that aims to optimally distribute the available bits to each frame. Initially when the encoder is fed with the frames it possesses no information about the input. While it would be obvious to us that the high-motion scenes or ones with high-detailed texture would require more bits, the encoder has no such knowledge before it actually reads all the frames.

Therefore, it is beneficial to scan the video to be encoded in full and collect information about each frame. Once the first *pass* is completed, we can use the collected data to encode the frames optimally. Some modern codecs such as DivX 5.2 allow multiple (more than two) passes to be executed. While there is some improvement with the additional passes, the encoder seems to converge after three or four passes so do not spend time for more passes.

Encoding with DivX

This section assumes you have installed DivX version 5.2.1 or later on your computer. Although the Pro version of the codec is described, users of the free version should be able to take out the additional information.

DivX was one of the first mature MPEG-4 codecs. To this day it has quite a large user base varying from beginners to video compression enthusiasts and movie studios. DivX was also the first "brand" to appear on standalone players. DivXNetworks (the creator of DivX) has set up a certification program to guarantee that a given device will be able to play a DivX-encoded video and vice versa. The program is based on four profiles:

1. Handheld profile
2. Portable profile
3. Home theater
4. High Definition

These four profiles control the maximum values allowed for the following parameters:

- Frame size
- Bitrate
- Frame rate

A device certified with the home theater profile will be able to playback any videos encoded with that profile or lower. Not adhering to any of the DivX profiles will mean that the video *might not* be playable on those devices. However if you are only interested on playback on a PC platform, the only limiting factor is the processing power of the CPU. Let's now see how we can configure DivX to our preferred settings.

Once you have opened a video in VirtualDub, select Video | Compression and select the DivX codec from the list. Then press Configure. On the resulting dialog, press Select DivX Certified Profile and do one of the following:

- Select the profile of the device you are targeting.
- Uncheck the DivX Certified box to use custom settings. None of the profiles allow the use of multiple B-frames, quarter pixel, or global motion compensation (**GMC**).

Press Next. The following updated dialog will appear:

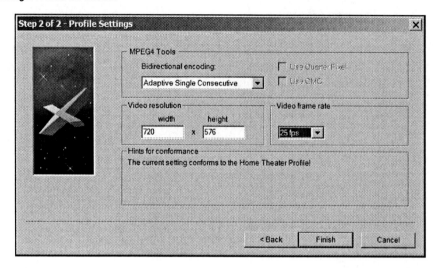

If you have used a custom profile, the video resolution and frame rate controls will be disabled and you will be given the choice of multiple B-frames, Quarter Pixel, and GMC. In any other case, you will need to enter the dimensions and frame rate of the video for the corresponding controls. DivX will be able to determine whether the resulting encoding will adhere to the profile you have selected and advise you accordingly.

Two questions that are probably arising in your mind right now are:

1.   What are these extra tools and why are they excluded from the profiles?
2.   Is it not worth conforming to the profiles to use them?

They will provide some increase in quality under certain circumstances, but if you want to be able to play your videos on a particular device, it is not worth sacrificing the compatibility for a small increase in quality. Quarter pixel will calculate and store more accurate motion characteristics and increase the video quality at the cost of some extra bits. GMC is useful when there is global motion e.g. camera pan. They are excluded because they add to the computational complexity and memory capacity requirements and consequently add to the cost of the devices.

Click on the Video tab to configure some of the more advanced features of DivX:

* Enabling the Psychovisual Enhancements will result in increased perceived quality, but this is totally subjective.

* Do not enable Pre-processing; this is a smoothing filter like the one VirtualDub provides. If your source is noisy and you wish to smooth it a little to ease the task of the encoder use the VirtualDub filter instead.

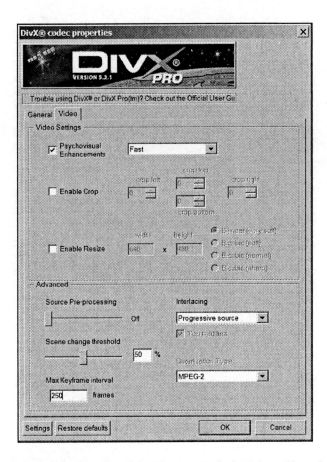

- If your source is interlaced and you have *not* de-interlaced it, select Preserve interlacing to encode it as it is. If you wish to de-interlace, use VirtualDub's filters.

- Change the max key-frame interval to about 10 seconds worth of video; 250 frames for PAL and 300 for NTSC.

- MPEG-2 Quantization will result in sharper, and in some cases, more blocky video. The default setting (H.263) is less blocky but also less sharp.

Go back to the General tab:

- The Encode Performance setting will control how much time the codec spends to find the most efficient compressed representation of the video. The default setting is standard, but if you have a fast CPU and want to stress the codec, select Slow.

- Enter the calculated bitrate in the corresponding box—this is the video bitrate. If you have chosen to have a custom profile, you will be given the choice of quality-based encoding where you select the quantizer used.

- In encoding mode, I recommend that you use at least two passes. Select Multipass 1st pass. If not, select 1-pass.

- Normally you will not need to alter this setting, but you can force the codec to spend more bits on high or low motion scenes by using the bitrate modulation slider:

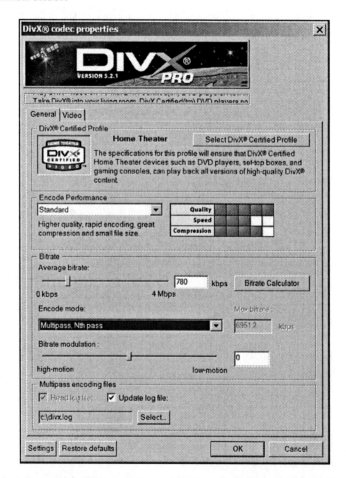

Click OK; you are now ready to encode. If you are only doing a single pass, just save the AVI as before. If you're doing more than one pass, the first pass will produce a dummy file full of black frames. It is easiest to use the job control for multiple passes:

- Select Multipass 1st pass in DivX settings; select to save the file, but add the job to the job control queue.

Go back to the DivX settings and select Multipass Nth pass. Select to save the file again and queue the job.

- Repeat the previous step for as many passes as you intend to do—there should be a minimum of two.

Once you have finished queuing the jobs, you can execute it and leave VirtualDub to it. I suggest that you try the above sequence of steps with a small (a few seconds) file so that even if you make a mistake you will not have to waste a lot of processing time.

Encoding with XviD

XviD's configuration (since it is another MPEG-4 codec) is along the same lines as DivX. Its open source nature has given XviD the reputation of the codec for advanced users and tweaking fans. The user interface has changed almost on every release of the codec; sometimes to accommodate new features and sometimes just to give a fresh and easier feel. This section will be based on XviD 1.0 (the golden release), but even if you have a different version the options will be similar.

Launch VirtualDub, load a video file, and open the compression dialog (Video | Compression). Then select the XviD codec and press Configure. The following dialog will appear:

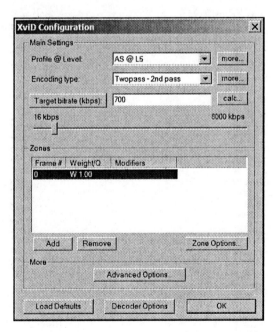

At the top you can see a profile/level selector; these profiles do *not* correspond nor are they similar in any way to the DivX profiles we saw earlier! They are in fact MPEG-4

profiles and allow different combinations of MPEG-4 tools, bitrates, and resolutions to be used. Without going into too much detail, the default AS @ L5 setting should suffice for most of your encodings. If you want to find out more about the different profiles and levels, look at the MPEG-4 standard, drafts of which are available online.

The second control allows you to select single or multiple pass; XviD allows up to two passes currently. If you select single pass, you can select the encoding quality via a quantizer or bitrate constraint. In the latter case, it will only be an estimate, as the codec does not have prior knowledge of the content as in two-pass encoding. If you select two-pass encoding, you will be able to set the target bitrate or *filesize*; this would save you some calculations. In contrast to DivX, XviD does not allow a bitrate to be specified during the first pass, as it is purely a statistics collection process. Much like DivX, XviD has its own calculator—notice the calc button.

Press the button labeled More next to the drop-down menu with the profiles. You will be able to select quantization type, interlaced encoding, quarter pixel, global motion compensation, and B-frames exactly as for DivX. XviD offers one additional option—Adaptive Quantization. If this is selected, the codec will attempt to select the quantization matrix most suitable for each part of the video:

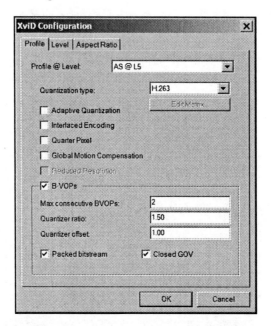

The tab labeled Level will provide information for each level that you select: namely, suggested resolution, maximum number of macroblocks, maximum processing & bit rate, and maximum buffer size. All this is possibly more information than you could ask for. The Aspect Ratio tab allows you to define a custom pixel or picture aspect ratio.

Press OK to go back and click on Advanced Options:

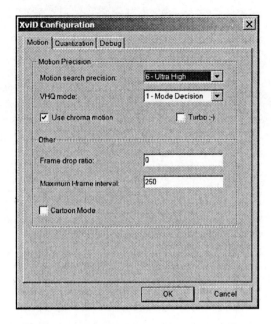

This dialog incorporates the interface for some of the more advanced features that are specific to XviD. Motion search precision and VHQ mode are two settings related to motion compensation: the higher the setting, the slower the encoding process and the better the results. Unless you have a fast computer and you are selective about your video quality, I would recommend sticking with the defaults. If you select chroma motion, the compensation will be done in the chroma domain to give better results.

The Maximum I-frame interval is the exact same setting as with DivX. Cartoon mode, as the name suggests, should enhance animation encodings. The Quantization tab allows you to select the minimum and maximum quantizer used for each type of frame.

MPEG-4 in AVI Interoperability

We have analyzed the whole interoperability issue and discussed where MPEG-4 stands. Even though MPEG-4 streams should be decodable by any decoder of the kind, this is not quite the case for MPEG-4 video wrapped in AVI files. This section will briefly explain why and how to overcome the problem.

Every video stream present in an AVI file contains a four-character identifier (FOURCC) that identifies the codec used to compress the stream.

On playback, this identifier is matched against the available codecs and a decoder capable of decoding the format is selected.

For example:

- XviD uses the XVID FOURCC.
- DivX uses the DIVX and DX50 FOURCC.
- HuffYUV uses the HFYU FOURCC.

Unfortunately, the FOURCC identifier is codec-specific and not format specific. In other words, there is no FOURCC to indicate MPEG-4 video. However, it makes sense for each codec provider to use its own identifier. As logical as this might seem on first sight, it takes away the interoperability advantages of MPEG-4. For instance, although it *can* DivX will not accept to decode XviD video because of the different FOURCC.

There are three ways to overcome this limitation:

1. Manually force one FOURCC for all codecs. Ideally, this would be an MPEG-4 FOURCC, but since the decoders would not accept this, it will have to be one of the MPEG-4 codec FOURCCs. This is a very bad way of dealing with the issue as it will once again leave the video file non-interoperable.
2. Convert the AVI file to an MP4 file. This is probably the best choice; many players support this. The only disadvantage is that currently no applications are able to edit MP4 files.
3. Install a decoder that will volunteer to play all FOURCCs associated with MPEG-4 video (see below).

3ivX provides a free decoding suite that allows you to play both MP4 and AVI files—it can be configured to accept DivX and XviD video. Ffdshow and FFvfw are also two very good free decoders with similar capabilities. Check out `http://ffdshow.sourceforge .net/tikiwiki/tiki-view_articles.php`. Finally, a very good application to convert AVI files to MP4 is MP4GUI, available from `http://mp4ui.sourceforge.net/`.

Compressing the Audio

To configure VirtualDub to compress the audio is a very similar process to that for the video. In fact, it's slightly easier as audio codecs have fewer options than video codecs. Most of the terminology is common between the two:

- The data rate is specified in terms of kilobits or kilobytes.
- Rate is controlled in one of the following (encoding modes):
    - Constant bitrate
    - Average bitrate
    - Variable bitrate

Audio is however, a one-dimensional data and therefore quite different in nature from video. Therefore:

- Instead of spatial dimensions we have a number of channels. Mono sound is recorded with one channel, stereo sound with two, and multi-channel audio with a variable number of channels (e.g. 5.1 Surround has six channels).

- Instead of frame rate we have sample rate—the number of samples recorded every second. Current state-of-the-art codecs are tuned to handle frequencies of up to 48,000 Hz, which is the sample rate used in DVDs. Audio CDs are sampled at a rate of 44.1 kHz. It comes naturally that audio that is sampled at a higher frequency will sound better. In the same way, higher resolution video retains more detail and higher frame-rate video is smoother in terms of motion. However, when you increase the sample rate you increase the amount of data to be coded and this makes it harder to compress the audio efficiently. Therefore, a healthy compromise is required.

We have already seen the VirtualDub audio codec selection and configuration dialog. Let's take a second look and notice where all of the above is placed. Launch VirtualDub, open your favorite sample file, and then select Audio | Full processing mode. The default setting is to directly copy the audio stream across whatever processing is performed. This is obviously because of VirtualDub's focus on video. Once you have changed the processing mode the Compression menu item will become available; select Audio | Compression. Select one of the codecs we installed earlier—LAME or Speex:

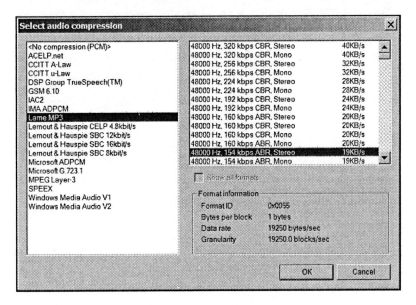

Let's take a closer look at the above screenshot. The entries on the right-hand side list describe every different format available on the encoder.

For example, the line 48000 Hz, 154kbps ABR, Stereo   19KB/s means:

- The audio will be encoded at a sample rate of 48 kHz. If that is lower than your input audio, it will be down-sampled internally by the encoder.

- The data rate will average at 154kbps approximately. For CBR, the advertised bitrate indicates exactly how many bits will be spent to encode each second of audio.

VBR modes are not popular for audio codecs as it is hard to position VBR audio chunks in AVI files.

- The audio will be encoded in Stereo—i.e. two channels. If this is less than your input audio, it will be reduced internally. Bear in mind that AVI (and therefore VirtualDub) does not support multi-channel audio.

- The data rate corresponds to approximately 19 kilobytes/sec or 19250 bytes/sec.

Multiplexing Audio and Video

Multiplexing is the joining or mixing of audio and video. If you have captured or imported a video then you would not need to multiplex audio and video—it has already been done at the recording stage. For most recordings the original audio will suffice, but let's look at how you can save, process, and re-multiplex the audio so that you can improvise. This process, as much as everything else, is very easy to perform in VirtualDub.

To save the existing audio from an AVI file (assuming you have launched VirtualDub and opened the video in question) perform the following easy steps:

- Select Audio | Direct Stream Copy.
- Select File | Save WAV.
- Choose a path and filename for the file to be saved.
- If you want VirtualDub to process the audio before saving it, select Audio | Full Processing Mode and then configure the audio processing as desired.

Once you have edited the audio you can reload it in VirtualDub in the following way:

- Select Audio | WAV Audio.
- Select the .wav file you have exported from the audio processing application.

Last but not least, adjust the audio/video interleaving as required:

- Select Audio | Interleaving or press *Ctrl+I*.
- Check the Enable audio/video interleaving box.
- Enter the audio skew correction value. If the audio is playing later than the video you should be using positive values and vice versa.

That's it! When you save the AVI file, audio will be processed and saved as required by VirtualDub.

Summary

This chapter rounded up VirtualDub's capabilities—you should now be able to run a full encoding job: from capturing to processing, multiplexing, and encoding. You are now fully aware of the possibilities, but feel free to refer back to the steps of each process. In this chapter we learned about the following:

- Old and modern codecs
- Interoperability—what it is and how it relates to you
- Where to get and how to install new codecs
- How to compress the audio and video
- How to use job control to automate jobs in VirtualDub
- How to manually calculate the total audio and video bitrate
- How to configure modern codecs
- How to use settings of modern MPEG-4 codecs like DivX and XviD
- How to multiplex audio and video

That's it! Good luck with your VirtualDub projects!

Index

Thank you for buying VirtualDub Video: Capture, Processing, and Encoding

Packt Open Source Project Royalties

When we sell a book written on an Open Source project, we pay a royalty directly to that project. Therefore by purchasing *VirtualDub Video: Capture, Processing, and Encoding*, Packt will have given some of the money received to the phpMyAdmin project.

In the long term, we see ourselves and you—customers and readers of our books—as part of the Open Source ecosystem, providing sustainable revenue for the projects we publish on. Our aim at Packt is to establish publishing royalties as an essential part of the service and support a business model that sustains Open Source.

If you're working with an Open Source project that you would like us to publish on, and subsequently pay royalties to, please get in touch with us.

Writing for Packt

We welcome all inquiries from people who are interested in authoring. Book proposals should be sent to authors@packtpub.com. If your book idea is still at an early stage and you would like to discuss it first before writing a formal book proposal, contact us: one of our commissioning editors will get in touch with you.

We're not just looking for published authors; if you have strong technical skills but no writing experience, our experienced editors can help you develop a writing career, or simply get some additional reward for your expertise.

About Packt Publishing

Packt, pronounced 'packed,' published its first book "*Mastering phpMyAdmin for Effective MySQL Management*" in April 2004 and subsequently continued to specialize in publishing highly focused books on specific technologies and solutions.

Our books and publications share the experiences of your fellow IT professionals in adapting and customizing today's systems, applications, and frameworks. Our solution-based books give you the knowledge and power to customize the software and technologies you're using to get the job done. Packt books are more specific and less general than the IT books you have seen in the past. Our unique business model allows us to bring you more focused information, giving you more of what you need to know, and less of what you don't.

Packt is a modern, yet unique publishing company, which focusses on producing quality, cutting-edge books for communities of developers, administrators, and newbies alike. For more information, please visit our website: www.PacktPub.com.

Printed in the United Kingdom
by Lightning Source UK Ltd.
104541UKS00002B/93-124

9 781904 811350